Windows 7

The Black Book

Sean Odom

This book is dedicated to my family whom I neglected each and every day I was writing this book. And to all those who have helped me in my career, to write, and publish 26 technical books in the past 10 years.

And to all those who read my books and follow my work. The kind words you send in your emails are appreciated. You can keep them coming to Sean@MediaWorksPublishing.com.

Also special thanks to I.T. Dream Team (ITDreamTeam.com) who voted me the most sought after network administrator this year.

Windows 7 – The Black Book

The material contained in this Black Book are not sponsored by, endorsed by, or affiliated with Microsoft Corporation. The Microsoft logo, Microsoft TechNet, Bing.com, Windows 7, and all other Microsoft programs and logos are trademarks of Microsoft Corporation. All other trademarks are trademarks of their respective owners.

ISBN: 978-0-557-13764-0

MediaWorks Publishing has attempted whenever possible throughout this book to distinguish proprietary trademarks from descriptive terms by following capitalization and style used by their respective owners.

The publishers of this book are in no way associated companies whom distribute or previously distributed similar named books, including but not limited to the Coriolis Group, Paraglyph Press, Activator, BlackBook.com, Black Book USA, and The Complete Black Book Series.

Cover images licensed for print from Fotolia US.

About the author

Used by permission from ITDreamTeam.com

Sean Odom has been in the Information Technology industry for over 20 years and in that time he has written for such publishers as Que, Sybex,, Coriolis, Paraglyph Press, and now Media Works Publishing.

Along with writing, Sean has also mastered many facets of Information Technology. In fact the number of skills he possesses is virtually impossible to find in one single individual. Companies usually need to hire many skilled individuals to run their organization. Sean has the skills to handle them all.

He is a Microsoft Certified Systems Engineer(MCSE) and a Microsoft Certified Systems Administrator (MCSA). Along with that he is an expert at networking, an expert at supporting operating systems, an expert trainer, does web design, search engine optimization, is a certified physical cabling expert, and one of the foremost experts in network security and intrusion detection.

Sean is well known in the Search Engine Optimization (SEO) industry as well. Some of his techniques have been learned and put in to use by many others through books and news articles he has written. He has also been credited with starting an entire industry of SEO professionals and related businesses. Sean was one of the first to introduce SEO techniques and make it well known with the very first article on the subject in 1989.

Acknowledgements

I have to thank many of those who care about me the most. The ones that have said lately, "Even when I am home. I am not home." Also to the person who gives me a day job and has too much faith in me, Randy Bankofier. I must also include the people that support me at work. They include Mark Eames, Risa Fitzsimmons, and Alan Frazier.

Also I have to acknowledge a few really great friends and customers. Joe Smith, Rita Peters, and Bruce Winkel from the Quimby Corporation, Sherri Whiteman at One Source Office Interiors, Ramzan Magomedov and Chris Brynelson at Griffon May, Jennifer Pittsley at Shaker Square, Marc Christenson at Metro New Holland Tractors, Ken Gregg at Sliding Thru Productions, Neal Ice at A Bobcat Excavations, Rick and Kolbi Anderson who feed me my favorite Lemon Grass Clam Chowder at "Typhoon!" Restaurants.

Also, I need to thank the entire team that worked together to write, edit, and get this book on the shelves in the limited amount of time we had to do it. My name is on the cover but it took dozens of people, sleepless nights to make our deadlines.

INDEX

Introduction

This book is for anyone planning to install, configure, or use Windows 7 as a standalone PC or in a domain environment. We cover it all. It is easily understood and in a step by step format with over 300 screenshots, figures, and tables.

It is recommended from a beginner's level all the way to advanced experience with previous windows versions. If you have never made custom modifications to a Windows operating system or have experience with modifying a registry, you should have no problems understanding this book.

Now that we have gotten that out of the way, let's get down to how this book is constructed.

Windows 7 is Microsoft's newest operating system. There are many changes and if you are used to Microsoft XP (Not in Classic Mode) and have graduated to Vista, you will find the stepping stones to this operating system much easier. However, if you are making the jump from Windows 2000 or Windows XP in Classic Mode, some of the changes will be a difficult adjustment.

We make this book pretty easy to understand for just about everyone. We have taken the time to really understand each picture and what you are looking at. When there are multiple icons on the screen, we describe what you are looking at, and give you pointers as shown below in figure I.1, showing the alerts flag on the new Superbar. Each screenshot or picture is labeled with a description and call out to the picture. Such as this one in I.1. (Introduction.Picture Number)

Figure X.X

And also here I this example where the item we are describing is highlighted here in figure I.2.

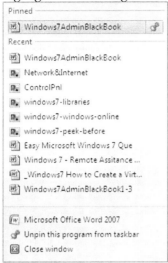

Figure I.2

Occasionally, a screen is really cluttered and so we will point out all the significant factors of that screen as shown in figure I.3.

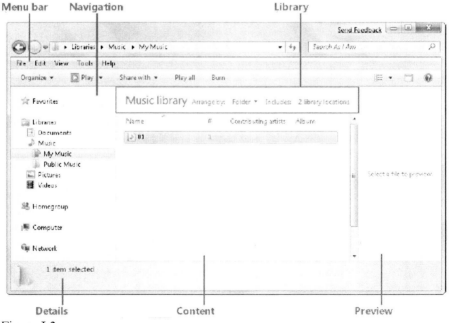

Figure I.3

Once we get past the installation portion in chapter 1, we will start with how the basic features are used and configured. Then we will talk about more technical aspects and how to use and configure those. There are actually thousands of customizations you can configure. This book only scratches the surface of the features most likely used in business.

Windows 7 operating system (OS) is packed with new features especially in the Enterprise and Ultimate versions. Such as:

- DirectAccess: Gives mobile users seamless access to corporate networks without a need to VPN.

- BranchCache: Decreases the time branch office users spend waiting to download files across the network.

- Federated Search: Find information in remote repositories, including SharePoint sites, and many others with a new simple user interface.

- BitLocker and BitLocker To Go: Helps to protect data on PCs and removable drives, with manageability to enforce encryption and backup of recovery keys.

- AppLocker: Specifies what software is allowed to run on a user's PCs through centrally managed but flexible Group Policies.

- Virtual desktop infrastructure (VDI) optimizations: Gives the user the ability to reuse virtual hard drive (VHD) images to boot a physical PC.

- Disk Imaging: Allows you to create a single OS image for deployment to users worldwide.

These are all available in the Ultimate and Enterprise versions of the software and will be discussed later in this book. But not all the features in this book are in every version. In the next chapter let's take a look at what features are available in each version, the upgrade path for legacy operating systems, and a brief description of some of the new major features of Windows 7.

Chapter 1 – Upgrade Paths, Requirements and Migration Strategies

Windows 7 Starter, Home Basic, Home Premium, Professional, Enterprise and Ultimate, along with the N versions for the European market each represent a simplification over the equivalent Vista versions that came out in January of 2007.

In Windows 7 each version is a superset of one another. If you upgrade from one version to the next, they keep all features and functionality from the previous edition. For example moving from Starter to Ultimate, each edition will supersede the previous, containing all of its features and adding additional components.

Microsoft is initially focused on the marketing and distribution of Windows 7 Home Premium,, Windows 7 Professional, and Windows 7 Ultimate. Rather than pushing all editions on the market at once, Microsoft is aiming the core editions at specific market segments to try and simplify the choices for consumers.

> *Alert:* One of the biggest mistakes made by those who purchased Vista was that they didn't realize you could not join an Active Directory domain using any Home Edition, Starter Edition, or Media Center Editions of Vista. The same is true for Windows 7 versions as well.

Although figure 1.1 on the next page only shows three products, there are actually seven Windows 7 Editions: Starter, Home Basic, Home Premium, Professional, Enterprise and Ultimate.

Windows 7 comparison matrix from Microsoft's website:
http://www.Microsoft.com/windows/windows-7/compare-editions/default.aspx

Compare editions

| Compare editions | Compare versions | Top 10 reasons |

Compare   Starter   Home Premium   Professional   Ultimate

Choose the Windows 7 edition that is best for you

Installing Windows 7? Read this first. ⑦

Features

	Windows 7 Home Premium	Windows 7 Professional	Windows 7 Ultimate
	Buy now	Buy now	Buy now
Estimated Retail Pricing (ERP) for upgrade license.	$119.99	$199.99	$219.99
Make the things you do every day easier with improved desktop navigation. ⑦	✓	✓	✓
Start programs faster and more easily, and quickly find ⑦ the documents you use most often.	✓	✓	✓
Make your web experience faster, easier and safer than ever with Internet Explorer 8. ⑦	✓	✓	✓
Watch, pause, rewind, and record TV ⑦ on your PC.	✓	✓	✓
Easily create a home network and connect your PCs to a printer with HomeGroup. ⑦	✓	✓	✓
Run many Windows XP productivity programs in Windows XP Mode. ⑦		✓	✓
Connect to company networks easily and more securely with Domain Join. ⑦		✓	✓
In addition to full-system Backup and Restore found in all editions, you can back up to a home or business network.		✓	✓
Help protect data on your PC and portable storage devices against loss or theft with BitLocker. ⑦			✓
Work in the language of your choice and switch between any of 35 languages.			✓

Figure 1.1

Version Equivalents

Windows 7 is designed to run on a very broad set of hardware, from small-notebook PCs to full gaming desktops. This way, customers can install the version of Windows 7 they want regardless of the hardware they already have.

Many people have Vista and XP and only want to upgrade to the equivalent version of what they currently have. So let us take a look at the different XP and Vista versions and match them up to the Windows 7 equivalent. We will also look at the availability (How you can obtain that version?), and the Windows 7 key features.

Windows 7 Starter

The equivalent of Windows Vista Starter and Windows XP Starter editions.

Availability: Worldwide, however this version is only pre-installed on new PCs by an OEM (original equipment manufacturer).

Features: Superbar (evolved taskbar), Jump Lists, Windows Media Player, Backup and Restore capabilities, Action Center, Device Stage, Play To, Fax and Scan, Games.

Windows 7 key features: Windows Media Center, Live Thumbnail previews, Home Group, users are limited to running only three concurrent applications.

Windows 7 Home Basic

The equivalent of Windows Vista Basic and Windows XP Home Edition.

Availability: Exclusively for emerging markets, only pre-installed on new PCs by an OEM (original equipment manufacturer).

Features: Superbar (evolved taskbar), Jump Lists, Windows Media Player, Backup and Restore capabilities, Action Center, Device Stage, Play To, Fax and Scan, Games.

Windows 7 key features: Aero Glass GUI, Live Thumbnail Previews, Internet Connection Sharing, Windows Media Center..

Windows 7 Home Premium

The equivalent of Windows Vista Home Premium and of Windows XP Media Center

Availability: Worldwide via mainstream retail resellers and OEM channels.

Windows 7 key features: Aero Glass GUI, Aero Background, Aero Peek, Aero Snap, Live Thumbnail previews, Multi Touch capabilities, Home Group, Windows Media Center, DVD playback and authoring, Premium Games, Mobility Center.

Removed features: Domain join, Remote Desktop host, Advanced Backup, EFS, Offline Folders

Windows 7 Professional

The equivalent of Windows Vista Business and Windows XP Professional.

Availability: Worldwide via mainstream retail resellers and OEM channels.

Features: Aero Glass GUI, Aero Background, Aero Peek, Aero Snap, Live Thumbnail previews, Multi Touch capabilities, Home Group, Windows Media Center, DVD playback and authoring, Premium Games, Mobility Center, Domain join, Remote Desktop host, Location Aware printing, EFS, Mobility Center, Presentation Mode, Offline Folders.

Windows 7 key features: BitLocker, BitLocker To Go, AppLocker, Direct Access, Branche Cache, MUI language packs, boot from VHD.

Windows 7 Enterprise/Ultimate

The equivalent of Windows Vista Enterprise.

Availability: Worldwide, but only to Microsoft's Software Assurance (SA) customers via Volume Licensing.

Features: Aero Glass GUI, Aero Background, Aero Peek, Aero Snap, Live Thumbnail previews, Multi Touch capabilities, Home Group, Windows Media Center, DVD playback and authoring, Premium Games, Mobility Center, Domain join, Remote Desktop host, Location Aware printing, EFS, Mobility Center, Presentation Mode, Offline Folders, BitLocker, BitLocker To Go, AppLocker, Direct Access, Branche Cache, MUI language packs, boot from VHD.

Windows 7 key features: Windows 7 Enterprise contains all the features offered with the next version of the Windows client.

Upgrade Paths

Unfortunately, because of features and compatibility issues, only a limited number of versions can be used as an upgrade path for newer versions. Attempting to upgrade a 32-bit(x86) operating system to a 64-bit(x64) operating system and vice versa will always require a complete reinstall.

Upgrading from Windows Vista to Windows 7

This is a tough pill to swallow for those who upgraded to Vista right away when it first hit the market. The RTM(Release to Manufacturing) edition of Windows Vista (the one released at the end of January 2007) won't have the option of upgrading to Windows 7. Microsoft's documentation indicates that upgrades to Windows 7 are supported only for Vista Service Pack 1 and SP2 editions.

When it comes down to Vista-to-Windows 7 upgrades, "Cross-architecture in-place upgrades (for example, x86 to x64) are not supported. Cross-language in-place upgrades (for example, en-us to de-de) are not supported. Cross-media type in-place upgrades (for example, Staged to Unstaged or Unstaged to Staged) are also not supported.

Let us now list all the remaining versions and whether an upgrade is available:

- No upgrade path for Windows Vista Starter (SP1, SP2), not even to Windows 7 Starter.

- Windows Vista Home Basic (SP1, SP2) 32-bit (x86) and 64-bit (x64) can be upgraded to Windows 7 Home Basic, Home Premium and Ultimate 32-bit (x86) and 64-bit (x64).

- Windows Vista Home Premium (SP1, SP2) 32-bit (x86) and 64-bit (x64) can be upgraded to Windows 7 Home Premium and Ultimate 32-bit (x86) and 64-bit (x64).

- Windows Vista Business (SP1, SP2) 32-bit (x86) and 64-bit (x64) can be upgraded to Windows 7 Professional, Enterprise and Ultimate 32-bit (x86) and 64-bit (x64);

- Windows Vista Enterprise (SP1, SP2) 32-bit (x86) and 64-bit (x64) can be upgraded to Windows 7 Enterprise 32-bit (x86) and 64-bit (x64);

- Windows Vista Ultimate (SP1, SP2) 32-bit (x86) and 64-bit (x64) can be upgraded to Windows 7 Ultimate 32-bit (x86) and 64-bit (x64);

- No upgrade path for Windows Vista Home Basic N (SP1, SP2), not even to Windows 7 N or E;

- No upgrade path for Windows Vista Business N (SP1, SP2), not even to Windows 7 N or E.

Upgrading from Windows 7 M3, RC, and Beta to Windows 7 RTM

Here we will look at the upgrade options for Windows 7. We will include the Beta and Release Candidate versions for those who tested Windows 7 before the official release:

- Windows 7 M3 to Windows 7 Beta in-place upgrade is supported;

- Windows 7 M3 to Windows 7 RC in-place upgrade is NOT supported;

- Windows 7 M3 to Windows 7 RTM in-place upgrade is NOT supported;

- Windows 7 Beta to Windows 7 RC in-place upgrade is supported;

- Windows 7 Beta to Windows 7 RTM in-place upgrade is NOT supported;

- Windows 7 RC to Windows 7 RTM in-place upgrade is supported.

Note: *Beta to RC paths are not supported by Microsoft Customer Service and Support.*

Special scenario upgrades exist where the user performs a 'Windows 7 to 'Windows 7' in-place upgrade as a means of repair (for example, upgrading Windows 7 Ultimate to Windows 7 Ultimate Repair In Place (RIU) which is supported as a way an upgrade path. This is opposed to a standard upgrade called a Windows Anytime Upgrade (WAU) which is also supported. WAU uses the Transmogrifier platform to transform a lower Windows 7 product to a higher Windows 7 product, for example Windows 7 Starter Edition to a Windows 7 Ultimate Edition.

ith Windows 7, just as it was the case with Windows Vista, Microsoft will offer two special editions of the operating system, the N and K SKUs, because it is obliged to do so by the antitrust authorities in Europe and Korea. In addition to these two editions, because of the objections of the European Antitrust Commission had related to the Windows – IE bundle, Europe Microsoft will also make available the E flavor of Windows 7, namely the operating system with the browser stripped off.

Improvements over Vista

The prospect of migrating an entire company to a new operating system is almost always a daunting venture. You'll need to make sure you get a return on the significant investment that you'll make in the product itself. The staff, time and resources needed to install it and work out the inevitable kinks.

Windows 7 has changed the name, look, feel, features, speed, and even the logo's to part ways with Vista because of the bad vibes that still resonate. Windows Vista met with almost immediate critical disapproval when it was released in January 2007. To be fair, Vista had many improvements over the XP operating system, including better security, file sharing, and search capabilities. But those were largely overshadowed by its shortcomings: constant security pop ups, excessive use of RAM, an overly aggressive User Account Control (UAC) feature, hardware incompatibility, and more.

Now comes Windows 7 and if the early reviews are any gauge including my review, Microsoft appears to have ironed out many of the issues that haunted Vista. In fact, some reviewers including myself feel it is the best Microsoft Operating System ever produced.

Improved security

Security is always a big issue with Windows. Witness the flurry of activity and tension that surrounds the typical Patch Tuesday. Windows 7 addresses the issue with a number of security upgrades. Microsoft has added the BitLocker full-volume encryption feature that came out with Vista.

The Windows 7 version still uses a 128-bit or 256-bit AES encryption algorithm, but is now more flexible and simplifies drive encryption by automatically creating hidden boot partitions. The result, users no longer need to repartition their drives after installation. And where Vista users required a unique recovery key for each protected volume, Windows 7 users only need a single encryption key. A new feature called "BitLocker To Go" lets users encrypt removable storage devices with a password or a digital certificate.

New improvements for IT administrators

A plethora of new options that make life easier for IT professionals as shown below:

AppLocker

This new feature is a control policy that allows administrators to precisely spell out what applications users can run on their desktops. It can also be used to block unauthorized or unlicensed software and applications.

Multiple Active Firewall Policies

This feature provides a big improvement over Vista, which automatically set firewall policies depending on the type of network connection you chose such as home, public, or work. Remote Vista users couldn't connect to multiple networks while on the road, or if someone working from home used a VPN, he or she couldn't apply settings to connect to the corporate network. Windows 7's Multiple Active Firewall Policies allows IT professionals to create multiple sets of rules for remote and desktop employees.

DirectAccess

A feature provides a secure way to manage and update individual PCs remotely. It uses IPv6 and IPSec protocols to create a secure, two-way connection from a remote user's PC to the corporate network. Users benefit by not having to manually set up VPN connections and IT professionals enjoy the ease of distributing patches and updates whenever remote workers are connected to the network.

Improved Windows Search

Is a new feature which allows for faster more thorough searches, and also provides IT administrators with better per-user policy oversight and the ability to manage resource utilization by controlling how desktop search accesses network resources. Additional improvements were the seek-and-find capabilities with Federated Search, which combines desktop, SharePoint, and Internet search methods and allows users to scan external hard drives, networked PCs, and even remote data sources. Another new feature enables the user to search for identical copies of files on drives.

Upgraded Windows Recovery Environment

A feature Microsoft introduced in Vista and was a replacement of the Recovery Console in Windows XP. The new upgrade allows users to perform a range of system and data recovery functions, including checking for defective memory, repairing boot-level startup issues, returning the system to earlier configurations, and other features we will discuss later in this book.

AeroSnap Desktop Feature

This is a new feature of Windows desktop. If you pull a window to either edge of the desktop, it automatically makes each screen half the screen and compares the two windows side by side.

AeroPeek Desktop Feature

This is another new feature of Windows desktop. In XP and Vista you had a button to minimize all the windows and see the desktop. The problem was that all the windows you had minimized you then had to maximize one by one. The new button to the right of the clock makes all the windows invisible when pushed. You can even click on desktop items and open them. Press the button again and all your open windows come back the way they were before you pressed the button.

Improved Backup Utility

This improved backup utility now gives users control over which folders they want to back up which was a restriction in Vista, which allowed backups on a per-volume basis only.

Windows XP Mode and Windows Virtual PC

These two new features address issues of incompatibility for applications designed to run older XP applications. You will learn to configure this later in this book. This shows Microsoft is intent on retiring XP as a supported product in the near future.

Speed, lower resource utilization and invisible open windows

Most users of Windows 7 will tell you that this new operating system uses fewer resources which make it faster than its predecessor, Vista. While that ultimately will depend on each PC's RAM level and processor capabilities, Windows 7 does boot up and shut down faster that Vista or XP, in part because the new OS loads device drivers in parallel as opposed to serial.

In addition the Windows 7 user interface is also less cluttered and the Control Panel and shut down features are less confusing. And those annoying security pop ups? Windows 7 adds a slider feature that lets users decide if you want those or not. YAY! It reminds me of the MAC commercials where the secret service agent stands between the PC and the MAC guys and tries to intervene every time the PC tried to talk to the MAC and vice versa. MAC had a field day with those commercials.

The taskbar has been redesigned to resemble the Dock feature in Mac OS X. The new taskbar features a customizable lineup of program icons that users can click on to launch or switch between applications. But Microsoft did one better on Mac Dock; right-click on an application icon in the taskbar and you get a list of actions associated with it.

For example, the Microsoft Word icon will present a list of the most recently opened files, while Firefox will lay out a list of your most visited web sites.

Finally, Aero Peek is a new feature that can be activated by hovering your mouse over a small rectangle on the edge of the taskbar. Your windows all stay open but instantly become transparent revealing the icons and features of the desktop.

Minimum Hardware Requirements

The hardware requirements for Windows 7 are relatively close to those for Vista. This is an improvement. Speeds of processors and RAM have greatly increased since Vista was released where the requirements have virtually stayed the same. Windows 7 requirements:

- 1 GHz or faster 32-bit (x86) or a 64-bit (x64) processor

- 1GB RAM (32-bit)/2 GB RAM (64-bit)

- 16 GB available disk space (32-bit)/20 GB (64-bit)

- DirectX 9 graphics processor with WDDM 1.0 or higher driver.

Note: Microsoft's free Windows 7 Upgrade Advisor can help you decide if your hardware will work; check it out at:
www.Microsoft.com/windows/windows-7/get/upgrade-advisor.aspx.

Driver and hardware support

Where this was an issue with CP driver not being compatible with Vista this does not seem to be an issue with Windows 7 which can use Vista drivers. There are some minor differences so Microsoft introduced the Application Compatibility Toolkit which allows IT professionals to inventory their applications and decide whether their applications are Windows 7-compatible. This way, companies can apply compatibility fixes if they are needed.

Windows 7 32-bit vs. 64-bit

Most people have no idea what upgrading to 64-bit gets you. You will see no upfront advantage if you are running 32-bit software on a 64-bit OS. You also lose the ability to run 16-bit software. If you have older DOS type application you should test to make sure it will work on and work properly on a 64-vit OS.

What you do get is more speed. More bits gets you access to more. The processor inside your PC communicates with your system memory (RAM). Thus, the maximum amount of memory a 32-bit processor can address is 4 gigabytes. 64-bit processors can address 17,179,869,184 gigabytes (16 exabytes) of RAM.

Most people will use Windows 7 64-bit to address the increasing demands for more RAM. But while 64-bit Windows 7 can run most 32-bit applications without a problem, it's not compatible with 32-bit hardware drivers or 32-bit utilities. This means you need a native 64-bit driver for every device on your PC which unless your PC and all your attached components have drivers to support 64-bit, finding support for all your hardware may be a bit of a challenge., especially on older computers.

The major benefit? 64-bit software running on 64-bit Windows 7 runs as much as 10% faster.

Now that we know all this, let's move on to Chapter 2 and learn how to install Windows 7 step by step. It is not like the other legacy Windows Operating Systems where you could just put the CD or DVD in and choose all the defaults and put a password in.

Chapter 2 - Installing Windows 7

Installing Windows 7 is particularly easy, but keep in mind that if you try to do an upgrade from Windows XP it will be a waste of your time and it will error out and you will have to start over from the beginning. Also, check and make sure that the PC or laptop you are upgrading supports Vista drivers as they are compatible with Windows 7.

The first laptop I used to install Windows 7 was a relatively new HP/Compaq Presario. When I got done with the Windows 7 installation from XP, the spare video port, the audio, and NIC card did not work. After researching I found that the laptop does not have Vista drivers and the HP website showed that the laptop was not Vista compatible.

I installed the 64-bit and the 32-bit versions on the same PC. Visually they are virtually identical however, the 64-bit version installed in 18 minutes and the 32-bit version installed in 31 minutes, a big speed difference even with the installation. Let's first go step by step and install the operating system using the upgrade option from XP on this PC.

Upgrade to Windows 7 Upgrade Option from XP

This is funny. I just told you that it couldn't be done. But I wanted to show you the error in figure 2.1. It takes a while to get to this error so don't try it to see if it will magically work for you. You will just get frustrated!

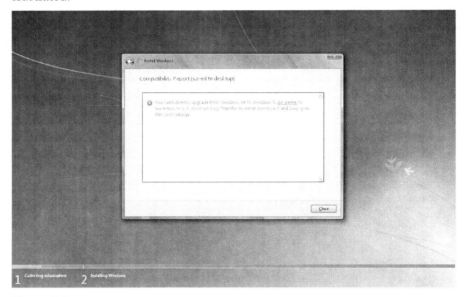

Figure 2.1

So now that you can see I have a sense of humor let's try this again using Windows Vista.

Upgrade to Windows 7 Upgrade Option from Vista

One of the coolest things is that Vista drivers are all compatible with Windows 7. I remember how long it took some printers and wireless devices to come out with Vista drivers when I did XP upgrades. XP drivers for the most part are not compatible with Vista. Let's go step by step. I am skipping the screen that asks you for the time and date and the password. I couldn't take screen shots of the screen. I took pictures with a camera but the editor said, "No way!" to my decision to put the pictures in the book because the quality made the book look unprofessional. Of course when I looked at it printed on paper I agreed with her. I will assume that you have seen these screens previously and can figure them out.

1. Insert the Windows 7 DVD.

   ALERT: The DVD does have an auto run but on the Vista install it would not auto run for me on two different PC's. I had to open the DVD drive in My Computer and double click setup.exe.

   NOTE: *If you are performing an upgrade, the Windows installation process will not delete the old version. It will rename the Windows Root folder.*

2. Click Install now on the Install Windows screen. If you by chance have an older computer without at least 1GB of RAM you can forget passing the "Check Compatibility Online" option. I checked it with my laptop that wasn't compatible and it still passed it. One of the PC's failed because of the video card and another failed because of deficient RAM. Figure 2.2 shows the initial install screen.

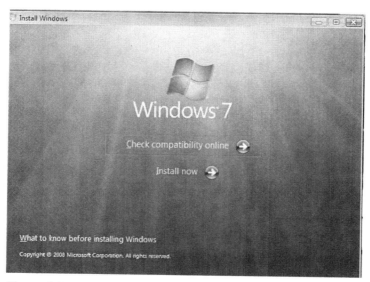

Figure 2.2

3. Press "Install Now" and the computer will begin the installation. As shown in figure 2.3

Setup is copying temporary files...

Figure 2.3

4. I chose the upgrade on this one as shown in figure 2.4.

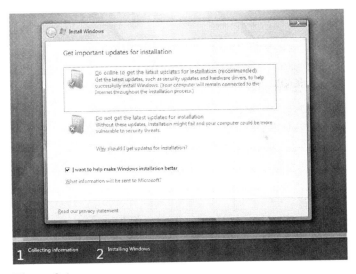

Figure 2.4

> **NOTE:** *Most of the settings will come over from Vista at the end of the installation. But if you are the I.T. administrator of a domain, you will want to read the chapter on Domain Administration and Configuration.*

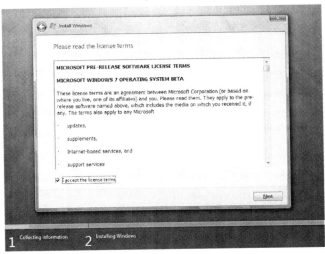

Figure 2.5

5. You will want to accept the license terms and click, "Next" as shown in figure 2.5.

> **ALERT:** *First it will copy the necessary files to the hard drive, reboot, and then start the configuration. It will be an automated process as shown in*

Figure 2.6. The PC may reboot as many as two more times before you are prompted for other options. On one installation I got a compatibility report. This is used to help you determine what may not work properly after the upgrade.

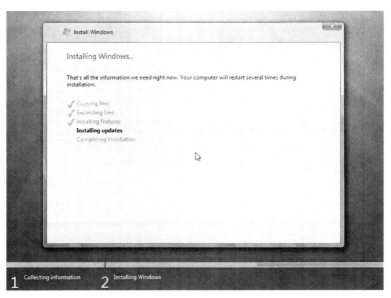

Figure 2.6

6. It will prompt you for a Windows login, password, and password hint. Windows 7 will use the login name you gave as part of the default computer name which you can change before continuing. It will also give you a screen that allows you to set the time and date before you get your brand new desktop.

Chapter 3 –Security and Networking

The Control Panel is the central configuration point of most of the user's system settings, security, networking, and the system settings in Windows 7. Unfortunately there is no longer an option for Classic View as there was in Windows Vista. So you're just going to have to learn how the settings are now categorized. Let's take a look at the settings and options of the Control Panel. Figure 3.1 shows the menu of the Control Panel.

You will see the Control Panel options in figure 3.1

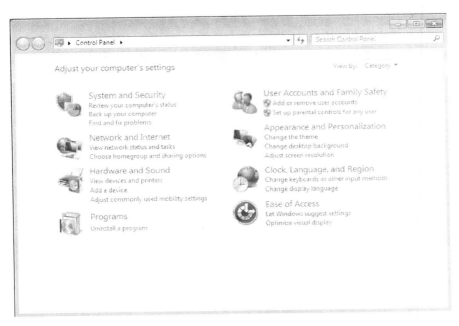

Figure 3.1

Let us explore all the Control Panel options. We will focus on those that are the most necessary to know for system and network administration.

System and Security

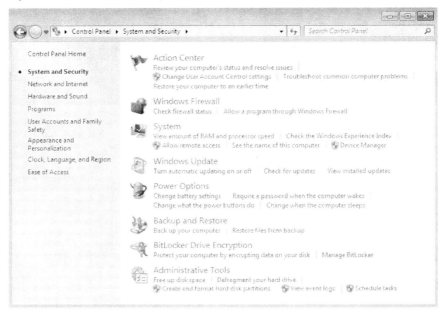

Figure 3.2

System and Security is the first option on the Control Panel as shown in figure 3.2. Here you will find several new items including the Action Center, the new enhanced Firewall, Windows Updates, a new feature called BitLocker, Power Options, Windows Backup and Restore, System Options, and Administrative Tools for the maintenance and installation of your systems physical storage and storage devices.

Let's take a look at these features one by one starting with the Action Center.

Action Center

This is where Microsoft decided that all the annoying little features that were included in Windows Vista could be turned off. You will find these items in the User Account Control also known as the UAC. This is also where you will now find the Windows Recover feature. Let's take a look at the options in this section as shown in figure 3.3.

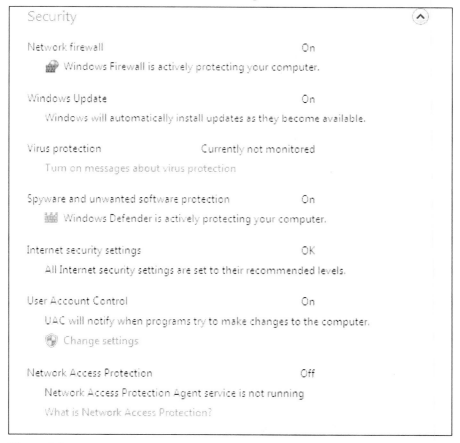

Figure 3.3

You can see from figure 3.3 that the first screen of the Action Center is actually a status screen with links to make changes. The first option as shown in figure 3.4 shows the firewall status.

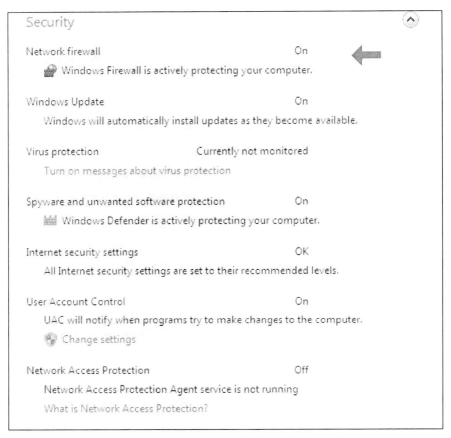

Figure 3.4

Unless you modify the settings the firewall, anti-virus, updates, or Windows Defender which is installed by default, Windows will alert you with a little flag on your Start Bar as shown in figure 3.5.

Figure 3.5

The next two options detect if your anti-virus program and Windows Defender are installed and turned on. In figure 3.6 you will see that

Windows Defender is turned on but I have not installed an anti-virus program on this test pc. Also shown is the Windows Update Service displaying that the settings are turned on. This is recommended. But if you are in a business environment centralized control and approval of updates after testing is recommended using Windows Server Update Service, and since Service Pack 2 was released it runs much faster and more efficiently.

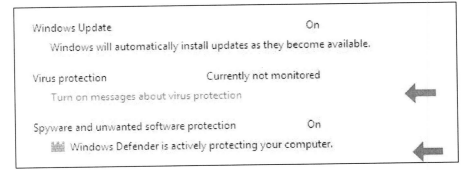

Figure 3.6

Next let's take a look at the Internet Security Settings which we will discuss later in the book. The Internet Security Settings as shown in figure 3.7 are the same that you see in Windows Internet Explorer when you go to Internet Options and modify the Security Settings. You will notice as you go through the Control panel that there are quite a few places to modify these settings.

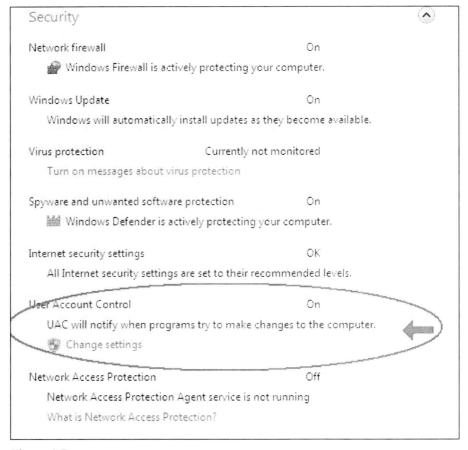

Figure 3.7

Figure 3.7, also shows the User Account Control. This is where you control all those annoying security pop-ups that came in the feature rich Windows Vista. These are the ones that every change you made came up and wanted an Ok or a password. Well good news. You get to modify these settings until your heart is content and make them go away completely if you'd like.

Figures 3.8, 3.9, 3.10, 3.11 show the four options available and when you will receive an alert.

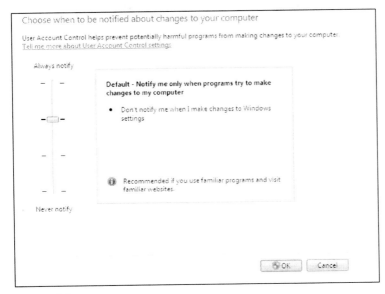

Figure 3.8

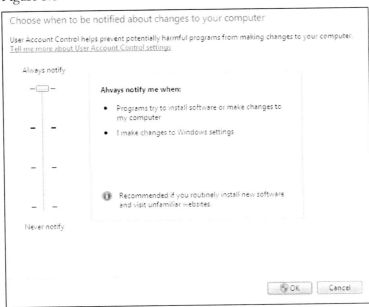

Figure 3.9

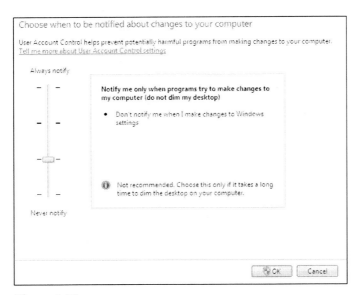

Figure 3.10

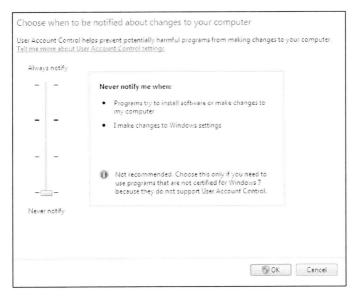

Figure 3.11

Network Access Protection (NAP) as also shown in figure 3.7 a few pages back is a platform that network administrators can use to help protect their network. We will cover this more in the Domain Connectivity section of Chapter 4.

Windows Firewall Configuration and Options

Well this is where this book will really come in handy. No longer does the Windows firewall pop up with a screen and give you three tabs to configure port names and type to block or unblock. It is a true firewall in the sense that it is feature rich and you have to configure rules just like a hardware router or firewall.

When you first click on the firewall it will tell you the different Home, Work, and Public networks you are connected to. Each one can be configured individually. This gives you a lot of flexibility when you connect to multiple networks.

There are several options available as you can see in figure 3.13 and 3.14. The first option is called, "Allow a program or feature through the Windows Firewall." If you need to allow a well known game or application this is the easiest place to go to allow it. Click and it will bring up a box with a check list. All you have to do is check the services or applications you want to allow and click Ok.

The second option is, "Change notification settings". Basically this gives you options to make the little flag on the Start Bar.

The third option is "Turn Windows Firewall on or off". This one is a no brainer. If you choose off, which goes against my recommendations, all the connections loose the firewall protection.

The fourth option to the left is called, "Advanced Settings" and is what we will focus on for approximately the next 20 pages.

Figure 3.13

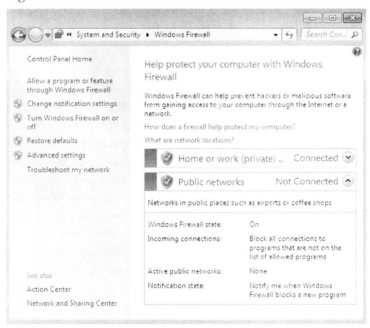

Figure 3.14

40

Windows Firewall - Advanced Features

If you are the systems administrator for the network and you support many desktops, you will really want to pay attention to this section. The firewall settings are now quite complex and the addition of inbound rules as well as outbound rules has really become quite complex for a novice. I foresee many novice users playing in here and screwing everything up. As a systems administrator the "Restore Defaults" link on the left will be your best friend to easily reverse what users have played with.

Let's first take a look at what we are dealing with in figure 3.15.

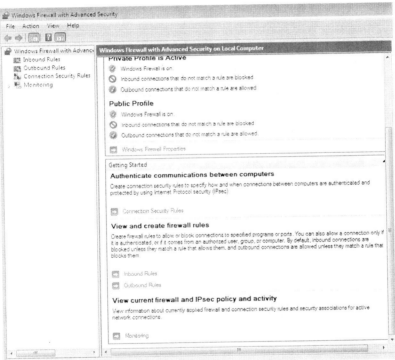

Figure 3.15

Aha! You were probably looking at the screenshot in figure 3.15 and thinking...um...ok I can deal with that. Well guess again. I couldn't fit the entire screen on the book page without a toggle bar because the writing would be so small on the options you wouldn't be able to read it just like you can barely read it now. The rest of the screen, which would be to the right of figure 3.15 is below in figure 3.16. Pretend the imaginary toggle bar extends below to that picture.

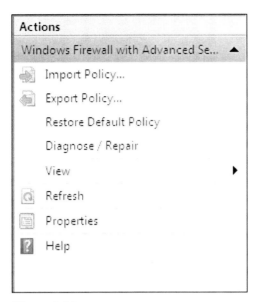

Figure 3.16

Let's now click on Inbound Rules and take a look at how they are configured.

Inbound Rules

If you click on the Inbound Rules link, on the left of the page you will get a display of the configured in bound rules. Those in use and allowed, have a green check mark. Those configured but not in use and those disallowed have a grey checkmark icon next to them as shown in Figure 3.17 below.

Inbound Rules					
Name	Group	Profile	Enabled	Action
Microsoft Office Outlook		Private	Yes	Allow
Microsoft Office Outlook		Private	Yes	Allow
BranchCache Content Retrieval (HTTP-In)	BranchCache - Content Retr...	All	No	Allow
BranchCache Hosted Cache Server (HTT...	BranchCache - Hosted Cach...	All	No	Allow
BranchCache Peer Discovery (WSD-In)	BranchCache - Peer Discove...	All	No	Allow
Connect to a Network Projector (TCP-In)	Connect to a Network Proje...	Private...	No	Allow
Connect to a Network Projector (TCP-In)	Connect to a Network Proje...	Domain	No	Allow
Connect to a Network Projector (WSD Ev...	Connect to a Network Proje...	Private...	No	Allow
Connect to a Network Projector (WSD Ev...	Connect to a Network Proje...	Domain	No	Allow
Connect to a Network Projector (WSD Ev...	Connect to a Network Proje...	Domain	No	Allow
Connect to a Network Projector (WSD Ev...	Connect to a Network Proje...	Private...	No	Allow
Connect to a Network Projector (WSD-In)	Connect to a Network Proje...	All	No	Allow
Core Networking - Destination Unreacha...	Core Networking	All	Yes	Allow
Core Networking - Destination Unreacha...	Core Networking	All	Yes	Allow
Core Networking - Dynamic Host Config...	Core Networking	All	Yes	Allow
Core Networking - Dynamic Host Config...	Core Networking	All	Yes	Allow
Core Networking - Internet Group Mana...	Core Networking	All	Yes	Allow
Core Networking - IPHTTPS (TCP-In)	Core Networking	All	Yes	Allow

Figure 3.17

Now let's click on the first BranchCache rule and take a look at the possible settings. Figure 3.18 shows the options available on the General Tab.

General Tab

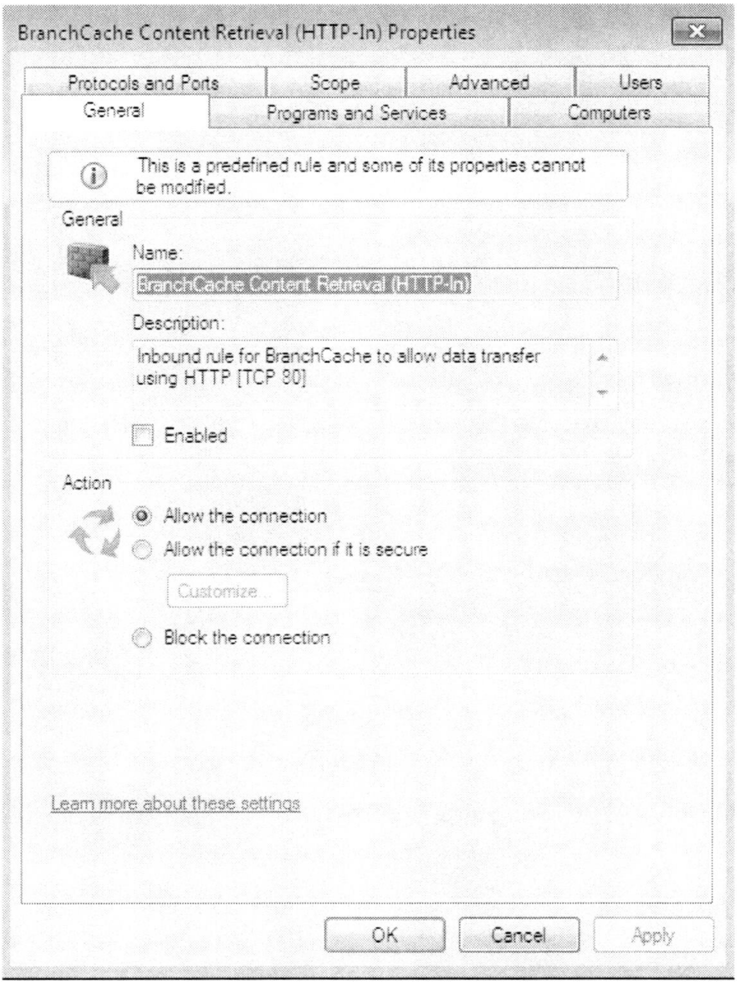

BranchCache Content Retrieval (HTTP-In) Properties

| Protocols and Ports | Scope | Advanced | Users |

| General | Programs and Services | Computers |

ⓘ This is a predefined rule and some of its properties cannot be modified.

General

Name:

BranchCache Content Retrieval (HTTP-In)

Description:

Inbound rule for BranchCache to allow data transfer using HTTP [TCP 80]

☐ Enabled

Action

◉ Allow the connection

○ Allow the connection if it is secure

Customize...

○ Block the connection

Learn more about these settings

OK   Cancel   Apply

Figure 3.18

The General tab allows you to configure the name, and a checkbox to choose to enable the rule. Next you can select the action that Windows will take for network packets, which match the firewall rules criteria. When you have multiple firewall rules defined, the order in which they are evaluated for a match depends on the action specified in the rule. Firewall rules are evaluated in the following order:

1. **Allow if secure** with **Override block rules** selected in the **Customize Allow if Secure Settings** dialog box.

2. **Block the connection.**

3. **Allow the connection.**

4. **Default profile behavior** (allows or block as specified on the applicable **Profile** tab of the **Windows Firewall with Advanced Security Properties** dialog box).

Alert: *A rule that specifies five criteria is selected over a rule that specifies only two criteria. As soon as a network packet matches a rule, its action is triggered, and it is not compared to any other rules.*

Programs and Services Tab

Figure 3.19

The Program and Services tab allows you to choose the services or programs that you can apply to this rule. The SYSTEM identified in the rule above indicates that the Windows operating system has access to this rule. If you press Settings you will be able to choose from a list of services installed on the PC. The Computers tab in figure 3.20 allows you to identify exactly which computers are allowed to use this rule and which ones will be blocked.

> **Alert:** Click **Settings** to match packets from all programs and services on the computer (the default), services only, or specify the service.

46

Protocol and Ports Tab

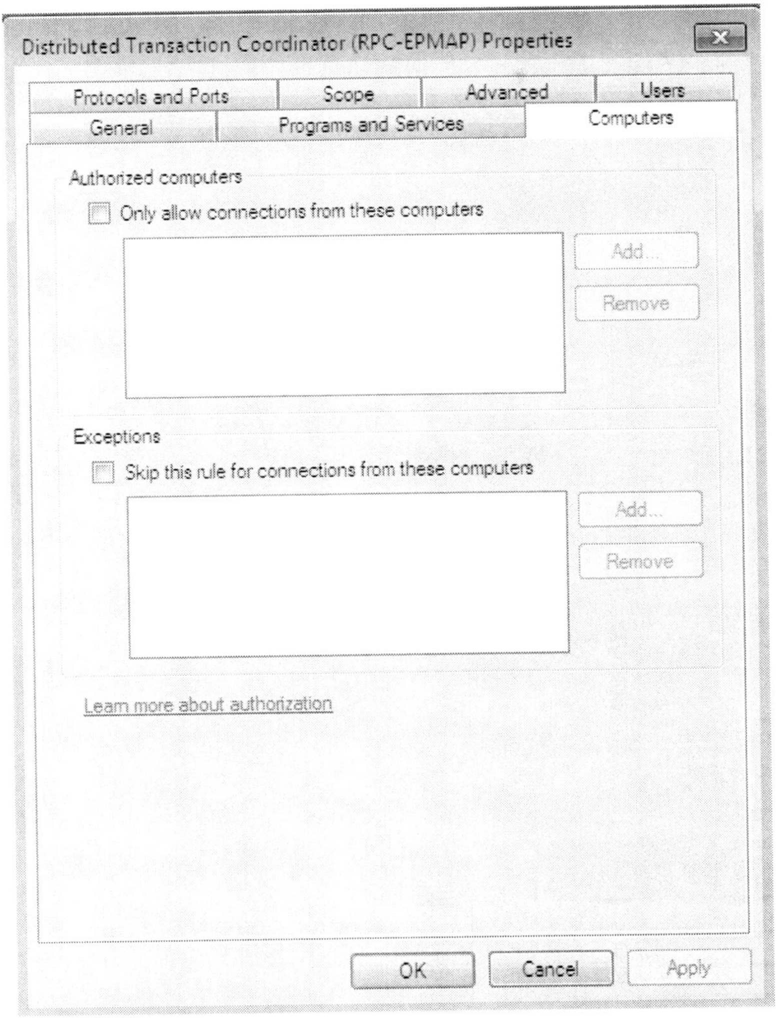

Figure 3.20

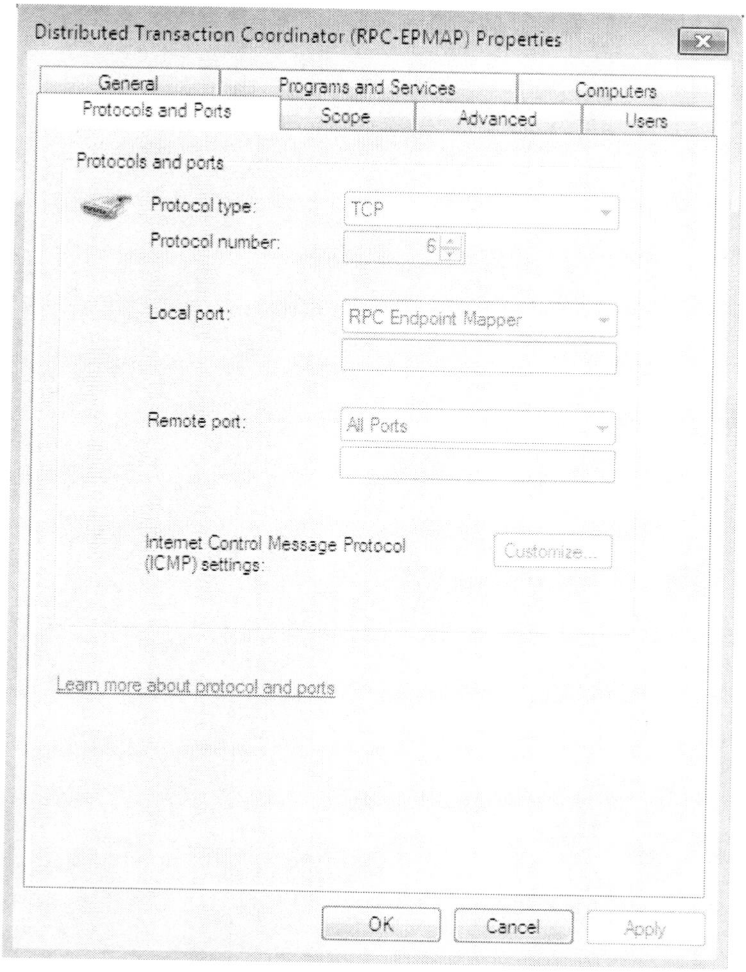

Figure 3.21

The Protocol and Ports tab allows you to identify whether the port number you are configuring is TCP, UDP, or GRE. If you are using dual multi-homed NICs the Remote Port is the port listened to on the PC and the Remote Port is the port on the inside that local network devices will listen to for the traffic. The Windows firewall will modify the traffic from the Remote Port number to the Local Port number.

> **SIDEBAR:** TCP or UDP protocol types allow you to specify the local port by using one of the choices from the drop-down list or by specifying a port or a list of ports. The local port is the port on the computer, on which the firewall profile is applied.

The following options are available for inbound rules:

- **All Ports**. Selecting this option specifies that all of the TCP and UDP ports for the selected protocol match the rule.

- **Specific Ports**. Select this option if specific port numbers apply. You can use a comma to add additional ports and you can include ranges by separating the low and high values with a hyphen.

- **RPC Endpoint Mapper**. Available for TCP on inbound rules only. This option allows the local computer to receive incoming RPC requests on TCP port 135 to the RPC Endpoint Mapper (RPC-EM). This option also enables RPC-EM to receive RPC over HTTP requests.

- **RPC Dynamic Ports**. This is for TCP ports on inbound rules only. This option allows the local computer to receive inbound network packets to ports assigned by the RPC runtime.

- **IPHTTPS**. Available for TCP only. For **Local port** inbound rules only. Selecting this option allows the local computer to receive incoming IP over HTTPS (IPHTTPS) packets from a remote computer. IPHTTPS is a tunneling protocol that supports the embedding of Internet Protocol version 6 (IPv6) packets in IPv4 HTTPS network packets.

- **Edge Traversal**. For UDP on inbound rules only. Selecting this option allows the local computer to receive incoming Teredo network packets.

   Note: *Teredo is an IPv4-to-IPv6 transition protocol.*

A list of port requirements for Windows PC's and Windows Servers are shown in Table 3.1.

Table 3.1

Port	Protocol	Network Service	System Service Logical Name
7	TCP	Echo	SimpTcp
7	UDP	Echo	SimpTcp
9	TCP	Discard	SimpTcp
9	UDP	Discard	SimpTcp
13	TCP	Daytime	SimpTcp
13	UDP	Daytime	SimpTcp
17	TCP	Quotd	SimpTcp
17	UDP	Quotd	SimpTcp
19	TCP	Chargen	SimpTcp
19	UDP	Chargen	SimpTcp
20	TCP	FTP default data	MSFtpsvc
21	TCP	FTP control	MSFtpsvc
21	TCP	FTP control	ALG
23	TCP	Telnet	TlntSvr
25	TCP	SMTP	SMTPSVC
25	UDP	SMTP	SMTPSVC
25	TCP	SMTP	
25	UDP	SMTP	
42	TCP	WINS Replication	WINS
42	UDP	WINS Replication	WINS
53	TCP	DNS	DNS
53	UDP	DNS	DNS
53	TCP	DNS	SharedAccess
53	UDP	DNS	SharedAccess
67	UDP	DHCP Server	DHCPServer
67	UDP	DHCP Server	SharedAccess
69	UDP	TFTP	tftpd
80	TCP	HTTP	WMServer
80	TCP	HTTP	W3SVC
80	TCP	HTTP	
88	TCP	Kerberos	Kdc

88	UDP	Kerberos	Kdc
102	TCP	X.400	
110	TCP	POP3	POP3SVC
110	TCP	POP3	
119	TCP	NNTP	NntpSvc
123	UDP	NTP	W32Time
123	UDP	SNTP	W32Time
135	TCP	RPC	msmq
135	TCP	RPC	RpcSs
135	TCP	RPC	
135	TCP	RPC	CertSvc
135	TCP	RPC	ClusSvc
135	TCP	RPC	DFS
135	TCP	RPC	TrkSvr
135	TCP	RPC	MSDTC
135	TCP	RPC	Eventlog
135	TCP	RPC	Fax
135	TCP	RPC	NtFrs
135	TCP	RPC	LSASS
135	TCP	RPC	Remote_Storage_User_Link
135	TCP	RPC	Remote_Storage_Server
135	TCP	RPC	
135	TCP	RPC	TermServLicensing
135	TCP	RPC	Tssdis
137	UDP	NetBIOS Name Resolution	Browser
137	UDP	NetBIOS Name Resolution	lanmanserver
137	UDP	NetBIOS Name Resolution	WINS
137	UDP	NetBIOS Name Resolution	Netlogon
137	UDP	NetBIOS Name Resolution	
138	UDP	NetBIOS Datagram Service	Browser
138	UDP	NetBIOS Datagram Service	Messenger

138	UDP	NetBIOS Datagram Service	lanmanserver
138	UDP	NetBIOS Datagram Service	Netlogon
138	UDP	NetBIOS Datagram Service	Dfs
138	UDP	NetBIOS Datagram Service	
138	UDP	NetBIOS Datagram Service	LicenseService
139	TCP	NetBIOS Session Service	Browser
139	TCP	NetBIOS Session Service	Fax
139	TCP	NetBIOS Session Service	SysmonLog
139	TCP	NetBIOS Session Service	Spooler
139	TCP	NetBIOS Session Service	lanmanserver
139	TCP	NetBIOS Session Service	Netlogon
139	TCP	NetBIOS Session Service	RpcLocator
139	TCP	NetBIOS Session Service	Dfs
139	TCP	NetBIOS Session Service	
139	TCP	NetBIOS Session Service	LicenseService
143	TCP	IMAP	
161	UDP	SNMP	SNMP
162	UDP	SNMP Traps Outbound	SNMPTRAP
270	TCP	MOM	MOM
389	TCP	LDAP Server	LSASS
389	UDP	LDAP Server	LSASS
389	TCP	LDAP Server	Dfs
389	UDP	LDAP Server	Dfs
443	TCP	HTTPS	HTTPFilter

443	TCP	HTTPS	W3SVC
443	TCP	HTTPS	
445	TCP	SMB	Fax
445	TCP	SMB	LicenseService
445	TCP	SMB	Spooler
445	TCP	SMB	lanmanserver
445	TCP	SMB	RpcLocator
445	TCP	SMB	Dfs
445	TCP	SMB	Dfs
500	UDP	IPSec ISAKMP	LSASS
515	TCP	LPD	LPDSVC
548	TCP	File Server for Macintosh	MacFile
554	TCP	RTSP	WMServer
563	TCP	NNTP over SSL	NntpSvc
593	TCP	RPC over HTTP	RpcSs
593	TCP	RPC over HTTP	
636	TCP	LDAP SSL	LSASS
636	UDP	LDAP SSL	LSASS
993	TCP	IMAP over SSL	
995	TCP	POP3 over SSL	
1270	TCP	MOM-Encrypted	one point
1433	TCP	SQL over TCP	SQLSERVR
1433	TCP	SQL over TCP	SQLSERVR
1434	UDP	SQL Probe	SQLSERVR
1434	UDP	SQL Probe	SQLSERVR
1645	UDP	Legacy RADIUS	IAS
1646	UDP	Legacy RADIUS	IAS
1701	UDP	L2TP	RemoteAccess
1723	TCP	PPTP	RemoteAccess
1755	TCP	MMS	WMServer
1755	UDP	MMS	WMServer
1801	TCP	MSMQ	msmq
1801	UDP	MSMQ	msmq
1812	UDP	RADIUS Authentication	IAS
1813	UDP	RADIUS Accounting	IAS
1900	UDP	SSDP	SSDPRSRV

2101	TCP	MSMQ-DCs	msmq
2103	TCP	MSMQ-RPC	msmq
2105	TCP	MSMQ-RPC	msmq
2107	TCP	MSMQ-Mgmt	msmq
2393	TCP	OLAP Services 7.0	
2394	TCP	OLAP Services 7.0	
2460	UDP	MS Theater	WMServer
2535	UDP	MADCAP	DHCPServer
2701	TCP	SMS Remote Control (control)	
2701	UDP	SMS Remote Control (control)	
2702	TCP	SMS Remote Control (data)	
2702	UDP	SMS Remote Control (data)	
2703	TCP	SMS Remote Chat	
2703	UDP	SMS Remote Chat	
2704	TCP	SMS Remote File Transfer	
2704	UDP	SMS Remote File Transfer	
2725	TCP	SQL Analysis Services	
2869	TCP	UPNP	UPNPHost
2869	TCP	SSDP event notification	SSDPRSRV
3268	TCP	Global Catalog Server	LSASS
3269	TCP	Global Catalog Server	LSASS
3343	UDP	Cluster Services	ClusSvc
3389	TCP	Terminal Services	mnmsrvc
3389	TCP	Terminal Services	TermService
3527	UDP	MSMQ-Ping	msmq
4011	UDP	BINL	BINLSVC
4500	UDP	NAT-T	LSASS

5000	TCP	SSDP legacy event notification	SSDPRSRV
5004	UDP	RTP	WMServer
5005	UDP	RTCP	WMServer
42424	TCP	ASP.Net Session State	aspnet_state
51515	TCP	MOM-Clear	one point

Active directory depends on the following services whose port numbers are outlined in Table 3.1.

Services on which Active Directory depends

- Active Directory / LSA
- Computer Browser
- Distributed File System
- File Replication Service
- Kerberos Key Distribution Center
- Net Logon
- Remote Procedure Call (RPC)
- Server
- Simple Mail Transfer Protocol (SMTP)
- WINS (in Windows Server 2003 SP1 and later versions for backup Active Directory replication operations, if DNS is not working)
- Windows Time
- World Wide Web Publishing Service

Services that require Active Directory services

- Certificate Services (required for specific configurations)
- DHCP Server (if so configured)
- Distributed File System
- Distributed Link Tracking Server (optional but on by default on Windows 2000 computers)
- Distributed Transaction Coordinator
- DNS Server (if so configured)
- Fax Service (if so configured)
- File Replication Service
- File Server for Macintosh (if so configured)
- Internet Authentication Service (if so configured)
- License Logging (on by default)
- Net Logon
- Print Spooler
- Remote Installation (if so configured)
- Remote Procedure Call (RPC) Locator
- Remote Storage Notification
- Remote Storage Server
- Routing and Remote Access
- Server
- Simple Mail Transfer Protocol (SMTP)
- Terminal Services
- Terminal Services Licensing
- Terminal Services Session Directory

Scope Tab

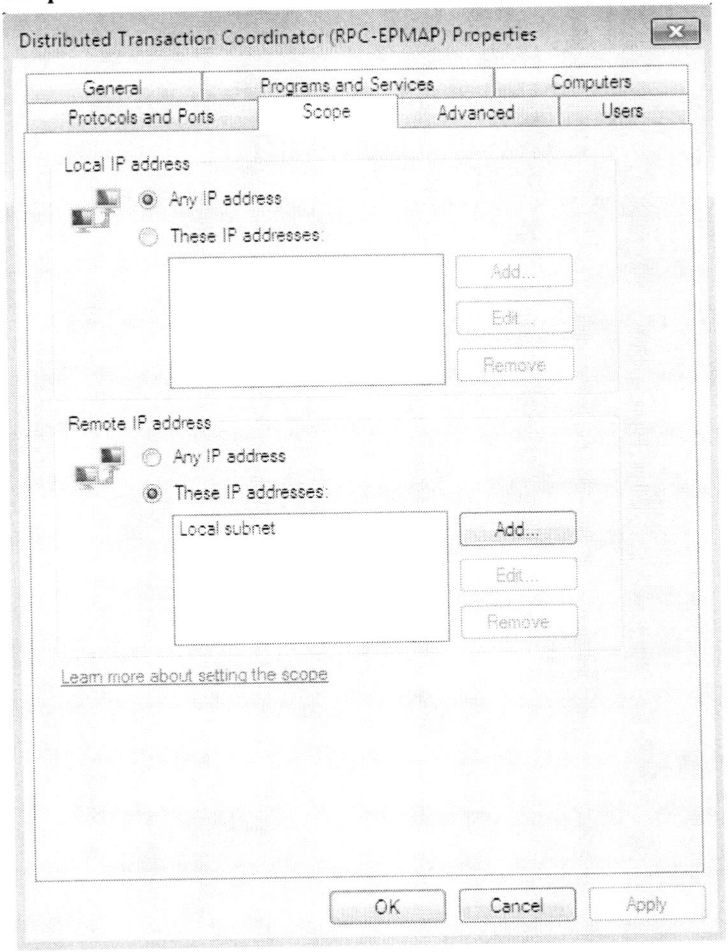

Figure 3.22

Figure 3.22, above shows the Local and Remote IP addresses that will be allowed by this rule.

Advanced Tab

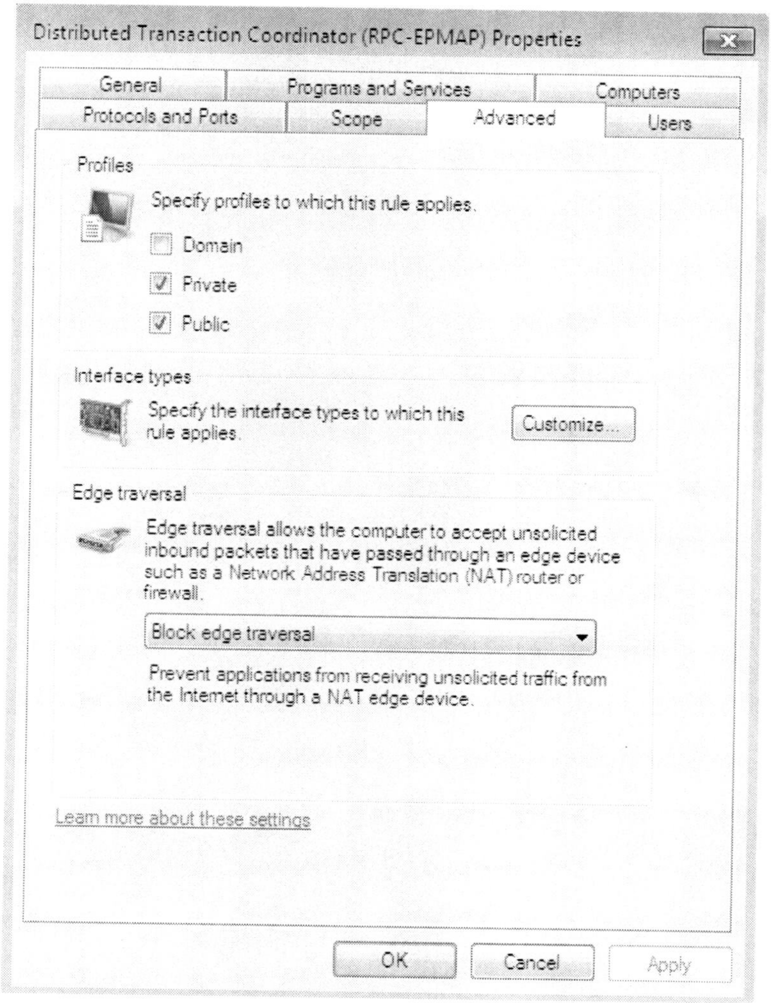

Figure 3.23

Figure 3.23, displays the Advanced Tab. In this tab you can identify profiles which are groups of settings you can configure. The following are descriptions of each option:

Domain: Applies when a computer is connected to a network which uses an Active Directory domain controller.

Private: This applies when a computer is connected to a network in which the computer's domain account does not reside.

Public: This applies when a computer is connected to a domain through a public network, such as those available in airports and coffee shops. This domain should be quite.

Interface Types: The Customize Interface Types dialog box let's you select all interface types or any combination of Wireless, Local area network, or Remote access.

Edge Traversal: Allows the computer to accept unsolicited inbound packets that have passed through an edge device such as a Layer 3 switch, router or firewall.

User Tab

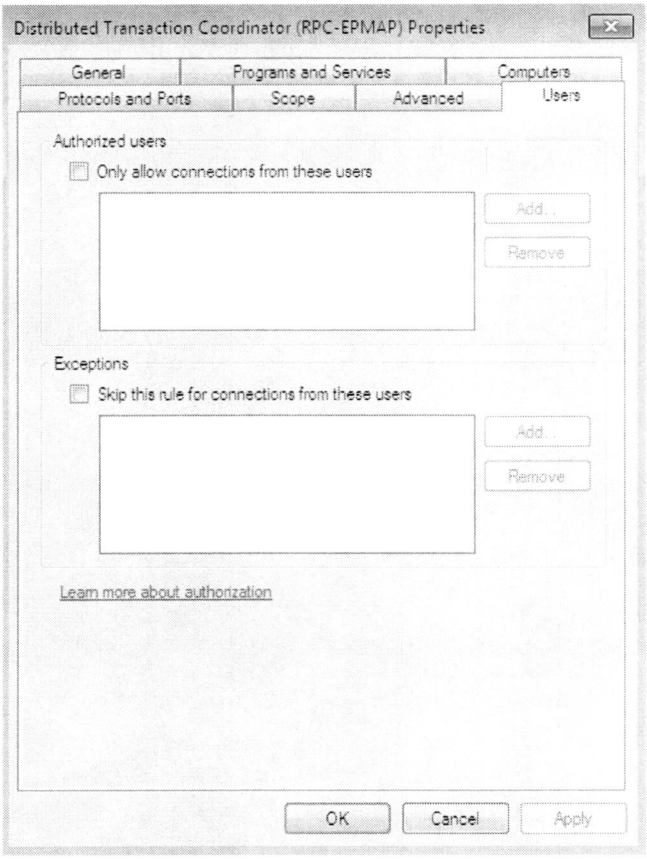

Figure 3.25

This tab is the easiest. In figure 3.25 you specify the users which will be applied to this rule. The firewall will accept connections from only authorized users you specify. Now let's say you identify a group of users but one of the users in the group is not allowed. You would put that user under the exceptions list.

Outbound Rules

Outbound Rules				
Name	Group	Profile	Enabled	Action
BranchCache Content Retrieval (HTTP-O...	BranchCache - Content Retr...	All	No	Allow
BranchCache Hosted Cache Client (HTT...	BranchCache - Hosted Cach...	All	No	Allow
BranchCache Hosted Cache Server(HTTP...	BranchCache - Hosted Cach...	All	No	Allow
BranchCache Peer Discovery (WSD-Out)	BranchCache - Peer Discove...	All	No	Allow
Connect to a Network Projector (TCP-Out)	Connect to a Network Proje...	Domain	No	Allow
Connect to a Network Projector (TCP-Out)	Connect to a Network Proje...	Private...	No	Allow
Connect to a Network Projector (WSD Ev...	Connect to a Network Proje...	Domain	No	Allow
Connect to a Network Projector (WSD Ev...	Connect to a Network Proje...	Private...	No	Allow
Connect to a Network Projector (WSD Ev...	Connect to a Network Proje...	Private...	No	Allow
Connect to a Network Projector (WSD Ev...	Connect to a Network Proje...	Domain	No	Allow
Connect to a Network Projector (WSD-O...	Connect to a Network Proje...	All	No	Allow
Core Networking - DNS (UDP-Out)	Core Networking	All	Yes	Allow
Core Networking - Dynamic Host Config...	Core Networking	All	Yes	Allow
Core Networking - Dynamic Host Config...	Core Networking	All	Yes	Allow
Core Networking - Group Policy (LSASS-...	Core Networking	Domain	Yes	Allow
Core Networking - Group Policy (NP-Out)	Core Networking	Domain	Yes	Allow
Core Networking - Group Policy (TCP-O...	Core Networking	Domain	Yes	Allow
Core Networking - Internet Group Mana...	Core Networking	All	Yes	Allow
Core Networking - IPHTTPS (TCP-Out)	Core Networking	All	Yes	Allow
Core Networking - IPv6 (IPv6-Out)	Core Networking	All	Yes	Allow
Core Networking - Multicast Listener Do...	Core Networking	All	Yes	Allow
Core Networking - Multicast Listener Qu...	Core Networking	All	Yes	Allow
Core Networking - Multicast Listener Rep...	Core Networking	All	Yes	Allow
Core Networking - Multicast Listener Rep...	Core Networking	All	Yes	Allow
Core Networking - Neighbor Discovery A...	Core Networking	All	Yes	Allow
Core Networking - Neighbor Discovery S...	Core Networking	All	Yes	Allow
Core Networking - Packet Too Big (ICMP...	Core Networking	All	Yes	Allow
Core Networking - Parameter Problem (I...	Core Networking	All	Yes	Allow
Core Networking - Router Advertisement...	Core Networking	All	Yes	Allow
Core Networking - Router Solicitation (IC...	Core Networking	All	Yes	Allow

Figure 3.26

Outbound rules such as those listed in figure 3.26, have the same menu choices. When configuring these rules you need to be thinking of what traffic you want to allow outbound instead of coming into the PC.

New Connection Security Rule Wizard

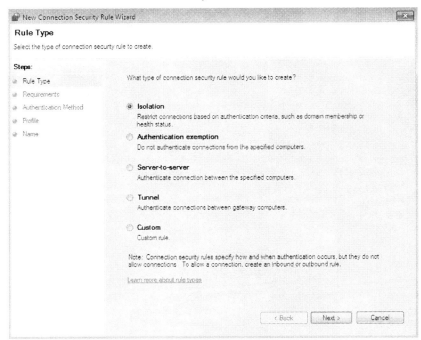

Figure 3.27

If you right click on Inbound Security Rules or Outbound Security Rules from the first Advanced Firewall link you will get an option for a "New Rule". Because they are so complex Microsoft has tried to simplify this process by creating a wizard. The first screen you get is shown in figure 3.27.

You have five options; let's review these options one by one.

> **Program**: This type of firewall rule is used to allow a connection based on an installed program or application. This is an easy way to allow connections for well known products such as Microsoft Office or other applications. It also gives you an option to link to an executable (.exe) file.

> **Alert**: *The program is allowed to accept connections on any port by default. To restrict a program rule to allow traffic on specified port numbers only, after you create the rule, you he will want to change Protocols and Ports tab rule properties.*

Port: Allows you to create rules based on a TCP or UDP port number or numbers. Use commas to identify another port.

> **Alert:** *To restrict the open port to a specified program only, after you create the rule, you must use the Programs and Services tab to change the rule properties.*

Predefined: Most well known programs and application already have ports and other information already configured in the Windows 7 firewall. All you need to do is select the name of the program and the Windows 7 firewall will enter all the port information for you.

Custom: It is recommended that you use this option only if you are an expert and none of the other options above can help you. This option allows you to setup any criteria for the firewall. But beware; you can also stop necessary traffic based on your entries.

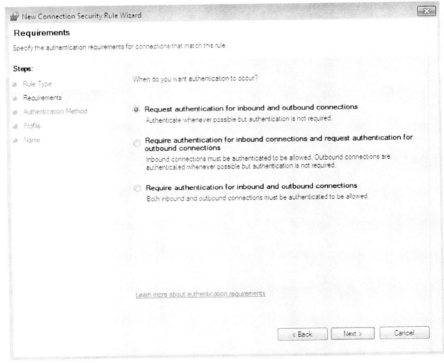

Figure 3.28

Figure 3.28, shows an authentication screen with three options to choose from for connection authentication. This only appears to secure applications or those using secure connections. The first option asks for authentication but does not require it. The second option requires authentication for inbound connections but not outbound connections. The third and last option requires authentication for every connection. You may also get a screen asking you for an authentication method.

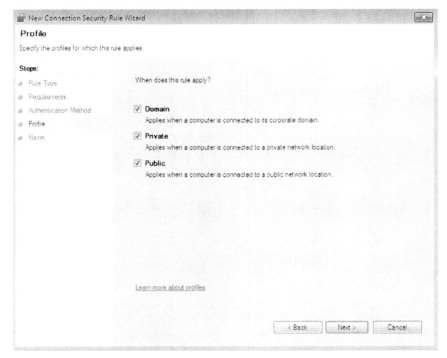

Figure 3.29

As discussed earlier in this chapter, figure 3.29, allows you to discuss the profiles which this rule will apply to.

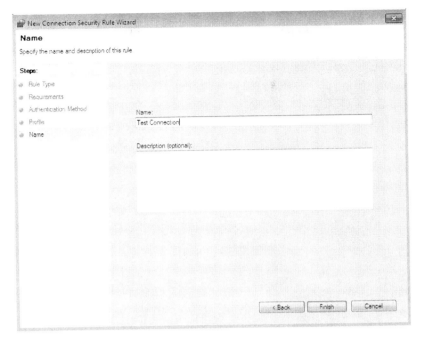

Figure 3.30

Finally, the easy part for most people, choose a short name for the rule
and a description which is informative enough that if another system
administrator needed to do some troubleshooting he or she would be able
to understand the purpose of this rule.

Firewall Monitoring

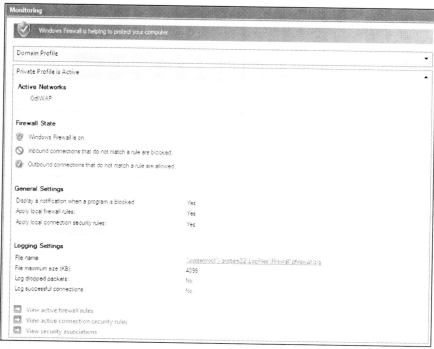

Figure 3.31

Firewall monitoring is making its fledgling introduction in this new operating system as seen in figure 3.31 above. In this section we are going to go through the configuration options you get when you

Click the Windows Firewall with Advanced Security Properties For Local Computer. In case I lost you and you cannot find the screen where to access the figures 3.32-3.35, you will find the Properties link on figures 3.15 and 3.16.

Domain, Private, and Public Profile tabs

By default the values seen on each of the profiles in figure 3.32, 3.33, and 3.34 are applied whenever Windows Firewall with Advanced Security uses each particular profile. Microsoft recommends that you enable Windows Firewall with Advanced Security on all three profiles.

Let's take a look at these settings in figures 3.32, 3.33, and 3.34.

Alert: *The firewall state is set by default to On. If you select Off, rules you have created or are using will not be applied or work.*

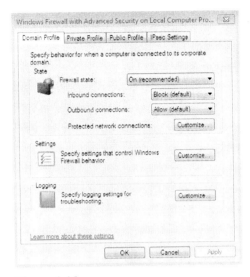

Figure 3.32

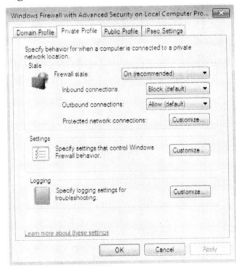

Figure 3.33

Figure 3.34

IPsec Settings Tab

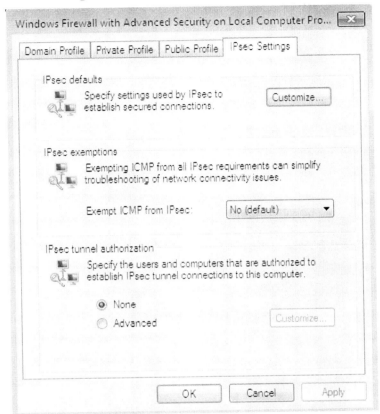

Figure 3.35

The tab shown in figure 3.35 is used to configure the IPsec default and system-wide settings.

Let's take a look at all the options on this screen:

> **IPsec defaults:** These settings configure the key exchange, data protection, and authentication methods used by IPsec to protect network traffic.

> > **Note:** *Click Customize to display the Customize IPsec Settings dialog box.*

> **IPsec exemptions:** This option is used to determine whether network traffic containing Internet Control Message Protocol (ICMP) messages are protected by IPsec.

> **IPsec Tunnel Authentication:** Most of the time this is used to identify users who are allowed to VPN into the server or

network. Here you identify user names of those who are allowed to make an IPsec connection.

Change Notification Settings

You can turn off the little flag as shown in figure 3.36 and notifications that the firewall is turned off with the settings shown in as shown in figure 3.37. This screen is available on the System and Security Menu in the Control Panel on the right side pane.

Figure 3.36

Figure 3.37

Troubleshoot Problems Menu

The Troubleshoot Problems Menu as seen in figure 3.38 is the last option on the right tool menu in the System and Security Menu in the Control Panel. Click on each item and it will scan your PC and list out any issues it finds.

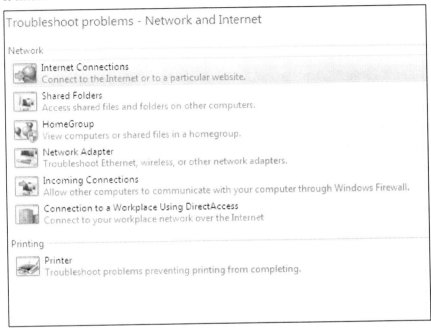

Figure 3.37

Configuring Network Connections

Since most networking protocols such as IPX and AppleTalk are gone and IP version 6 hasn't really caught on I will concentrate on how to configure IP settings. First, we will go to the Network and Sharing Center on the Control Panel as shown in figure 3.38.

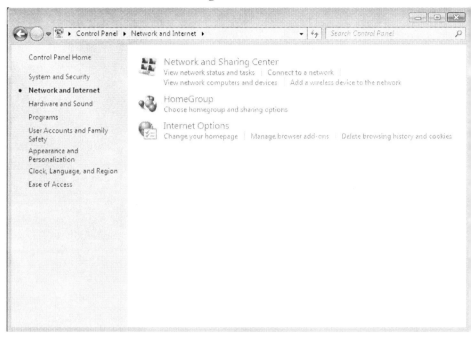

Figure 3.38

Figure 3.39 on the next page shows the networks that are currently connected. You will notice that I have a wireless network already configured called "OdiWAP". If you have a network connection that uses DHCP and you have plugged in your network cable, chances are you're already ready to go. We will manually configure an IP4 IP address after we look at configuring a wireless connection next.

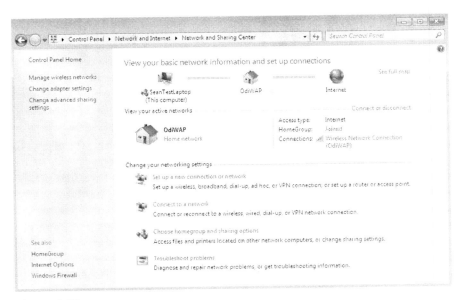

Figure 3.39

If you have a wireless adapter installed, most likely you can click on the wireless icon on your Start Bar next to the sound icon as seen in figure 3.40.

Figure 3.40

If you click on the wireless icon on the task bar it will display the available wireless networks as shown in figure 3.41 on the next page.

Figure 3.41

If you click on any of the available wireless networks it will either attach to the network or ask you for a security key for secure networks. If you would like to save it for future use, you will be prompted to specify whether the network is a Home, Work, or Public network.

Now if we click on the Network Connections link we will see the installed adapters. Notice the green status bars on the ones we are using in figure 3.42. I will click the Local Area Connection and see the Properties screen in Figure 3.43.

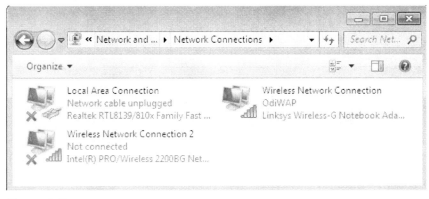

Figure 3.42

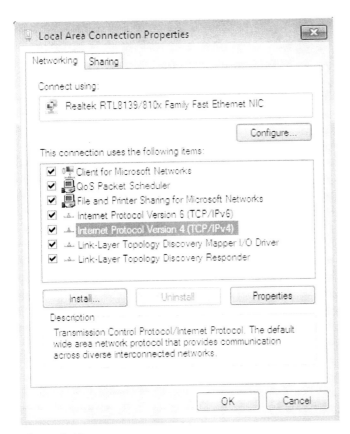

Figure 3.43

After we have displayed the Local Area Connections Properties screen
shown in figure 3.43 we will need to click on Internet Protocol Version
4(TCP/IPv4) and press Properties again.   The properties screen should
be showing as seen in Figure 3.44.

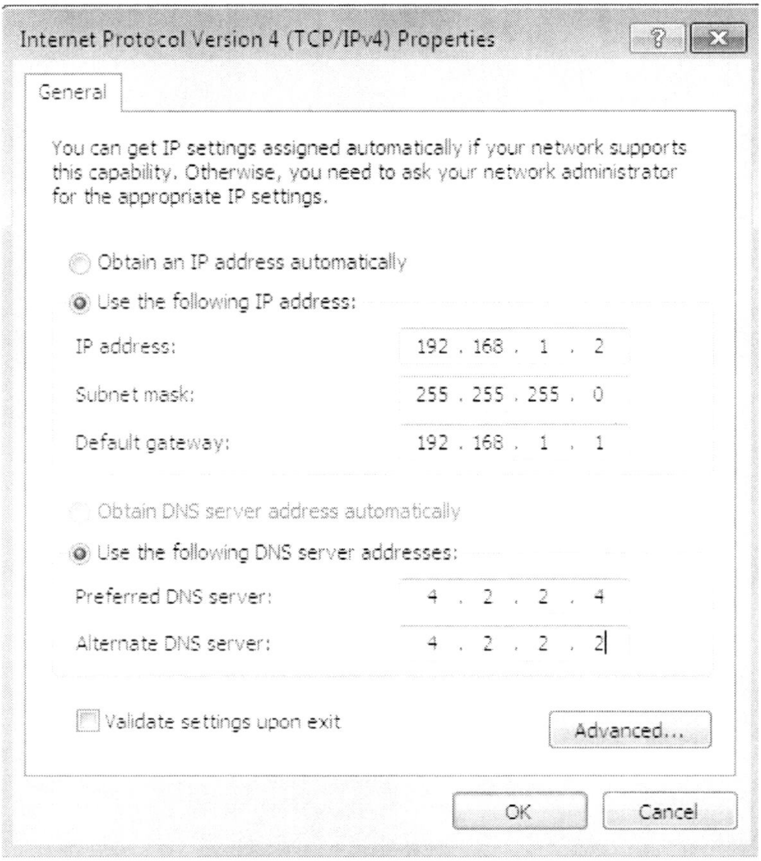

```
┌──────────────────────────────────────────────────────────────────────┐
│ Internet Protocol Version 4 (TCP/IPv4) Properties          [ ? ] [ X ] │
├──────────────────────────────────────────────────────────────────────┤
│ ┌ General ┐                                                            │
│ │                                                                      │
│   You can get IP settings assigned automatically if your network      │
│   supports this capability. Otherwise, you need to ask your network   │
│   administrator for the appropriate IP settings.                      │
│                                                                        │
│      ○ Obtain an IP address automatically                             │
│      ◉ Use the following IP address:                                  │
│      IP address:                         192 . 168 .  1  .  2         │
│      Subnet mask:                        255 . 255 . 255 .  0         │
│      Default gateway:                    192 . 168 .  1  .  1         │
│                                                                        │
│      ○ Obtain DNS server address automatically                        │
│      ◉ Use the following DNS server addresses:                        │
│      Preferred DNS server:                  4 .  2 .  2 .  4          │
│      Alternate DNS server:                  4 .  2 .  2 .  2|         │
│                                                                        │
│      ☐ Validate settings upon exit                  [ Advanced... ]   │
│                                                                        │
│                                            [    OK    ] [  Cancel  ]  │
└──────────────────────────────────────────────────────────────────────┘
```

Figure 3.44

My network here is in the 192.168.1.x network so I have configured it as shown above. This is an Intermediate and Advanced book so I won't go into the specifics of this configuration. However if you need to know about IP Addressing you can read either my CCNA Book from Sybex or my Windows 7 Professional Black Book by MediaWorks Publishing.

If you click on the advanced tab you can add additional IP Addresses, DNS addresses, or an additional WINS address as shown in figure 3.45 and hit OK.

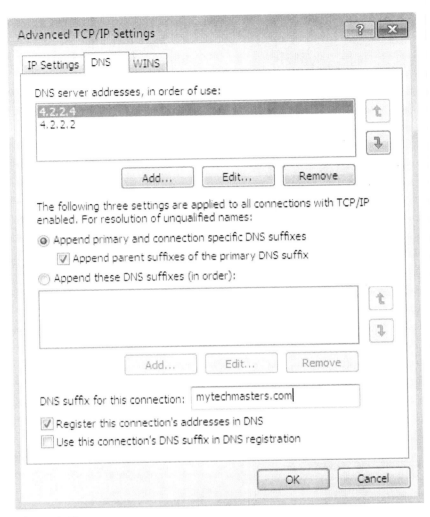

Figure 3.45

Before we move on to the next section I wanted to give you a troubleshooting tip. As networks have evolved switches as well as DSL Modems and routers have increasingly been placing ports in 10, 100, or 1000 Mbps with Full Duplex. The network card is set to auto by default and can lose connectivity due to the unmatched settings. To find where you change this, click on the Configure button under, "Connect using" where it displays the adapter type as shown below in figure 3.46.

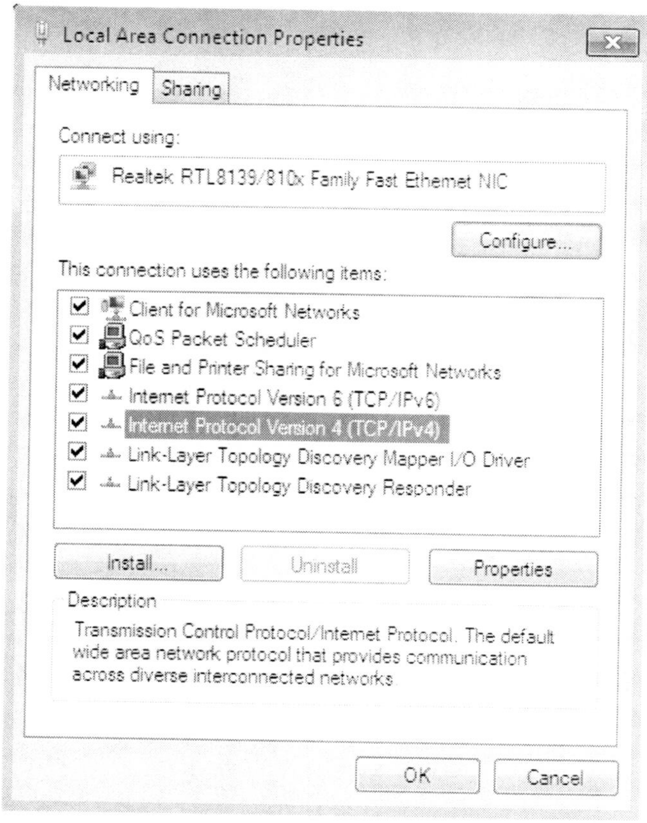

Figure 3.46

Under the Advanced Tab as shown in Figure 3.47 click the Line Speed/Duplex Mode and change the values to match the other side of the network interface. For instance, if I set the Cisco switch port the PC is plugged into at 1000 Mbps, Full Duplex, I would click the Value drop down and select that setting and then click Ok. You will temporarily lose network connectivity on the PC during this process.

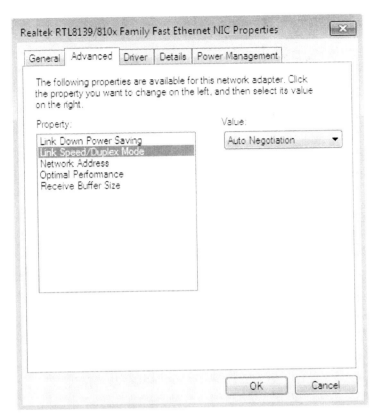

Figure 3.47

Chapter 4 Control Panel – User Accounts and Profiles

Windows 7 is the most secure version of Windows, Microsoft has ever developed.

Included in Windows 7 are some very good options for keeping your account secure. From passwords, to times your kids or workers can log in to Windows, all the way to the rating types of games and movies they can watch. This is all in an effort to keep your family as secure as possible.

In this chapter, you'll learn how to set up multiple users on a PC, select the right account type for different users, join a domain, enable Parental Controls, and much more.

We will also look at how to share your printers, hard disks and devices on the network. Then we will walk through the options you need to know to configure your Windows 7 personalized experience.

Configuring a User Account with Parental Controls

Under the Control Panel, User Accounts and Family Safety as shown in figure 4.1, you have the options to add, modify, or delete user or administrator accounts. There are also many other items from parental controls to controlling what applications can be run. In this section we will cover all of them.

Figure 4.1

I quickly added another account and made it a user account called, "My Kids" as shown in figure 4.2. After the account is created you can use this screen to change the account name, password, picture, or the account type. You can also setup the Parental Controls or delete the account.

Figure 4.2

I am going to click on Parental Controls as shown in figure 4.2. When I do this it gives me the option to choose the user to modify as shown in figure 4.3.

Figure 4.3

You will notice in figure 4.3, under the picture that there are no Parental Controls configured. Next, I want to keep my kids off the computer after 8PM at night and not let them use it until 7AM. So I will click on Time Limits and use my mouse to highlight the times I want to keep the kids from logging in as shown in figure 4.4.

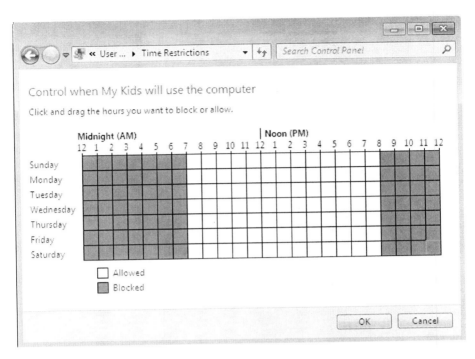

Figure 4.4

Now, there are definitely lots of games I would never let me kids see. In figure 4.5 I set the maturity level for games and movies played under the My Kids login to Everyone 10+. This means that all the games with a Teen, Mature, or Adult content will be blocked.

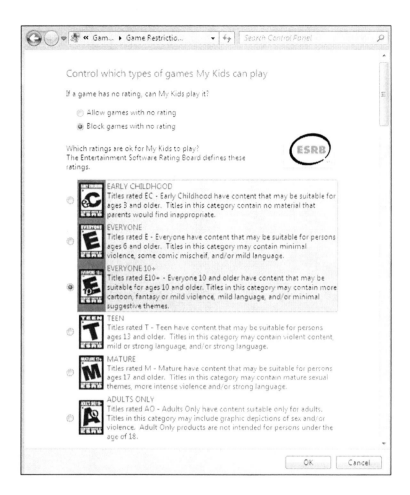

Figure 4.5

In figure 4.6 you see the Parental Controls which allow you to keep your kids from using any program or application installed on the PC. Any application that is not checked cannot be used by the user logged in as My Kids.

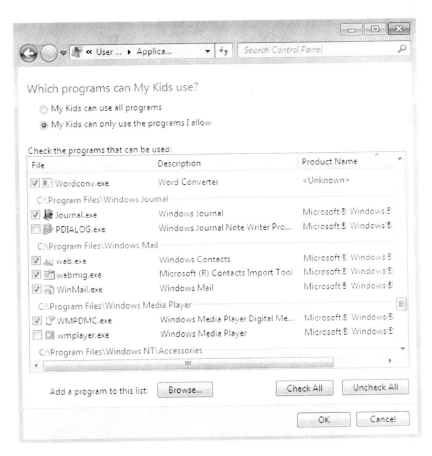

Figure 4.6

In the last screenshot in this section we will go back and review the changes we have made to the user My Kids as shown in Figure 4.7

Figure 4.7

Advanced Sharing Settings

Windows 7 doesn't allow your printers or data to be shared by default. In fact it doesn't even let your PC be discovered on the network. These are all options you have to turn on yourself. In figure 4.8, you see the Control Panel, Network and Sharing, Advanced sharing settings window. This is where you configure the options to share your printers, data, or allow other computers to see your computer on the network.

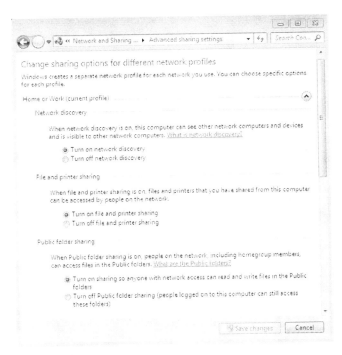

Figure 4.8

You will notice in figure 4.8 that you have the ability to turn on or off the ability to be discovered on the network, turn on or off file and print sharing, and turn on or off the folders you want to publically share.

Linking Your Online ID's

Microsoft allows you to link your online ID's from websites like Live so that you can get online content without the need to continuously log in to the sites. In figure 4.9, you see the Link Online ID's window found under the Control Panel, User Accounts and Family Safety, User Accounts. The link is on the left pane.

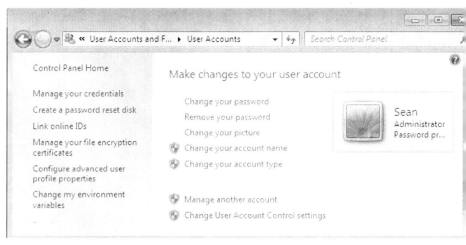

Figure 4.9

After you select Link online ID's you will see a list of the possible users that you can link ID's for. If there is only one account as I have configured you will immediately get the screen as shown in figure 4.10. Notice the Windows Live icon allowing you to link your Windows Live ID.

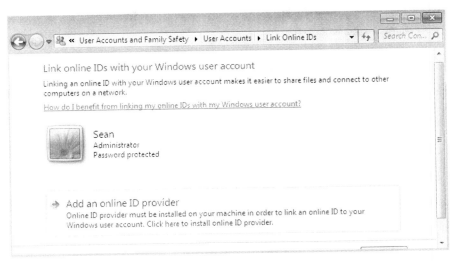

Figure 4.10

You will immediately be redirected to the Internet to sign in and allow your Windows Live ID as shown in figure 4.11. We were given a rereleased copy of Windows 7 Enterprise which only has Windows Live as options. Microsoft however intends to add Bing, MSN and other logins as well.

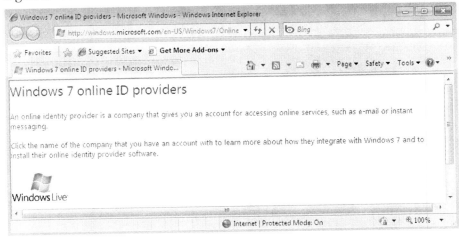

Figure 4.11

Joining a Domain

If you belong to a company, most likely you will be joining a domain.
Where you configure this is kind of hidden if you are used to Windows
XP and or previous versions.

Under System and Security in the Control Panel you will find the System
link. Click on that and you will see the screen below in figure 4.12.
Notice I am currently in a Workgroup.

Figure 4.12

But in order to get all the benefits of a domain we have to join an Active
Directory Domain. First click on Change settings and the screen in figure
4.13 will appear. Now this looks similar to the one in Windows XP.

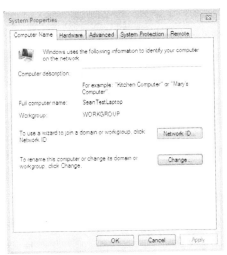

Figure 4.13

It gives us the computer name and then Workgroup we are in. Next let's click on Change and we will get the screen shown in figure 4.14.

Figure 4.14

When you have entered your domain name and clicked on the Domain radio button you will get a popup which requires a member of the Domain Admins group to enter their credentials to join as shown in figure 4.15.

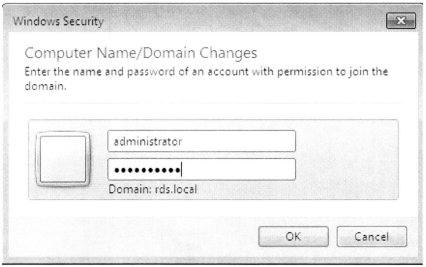

Figure 4.15

You will then get a popup the says "Welcome to the <Your Domain>." as shown in figure 4.16.

Figure 4.16

Normally in a Windows book it would stop here and tell you to do a reboot. But this is not a certification book, it is a real world guide and before I reboot I go one step further to save me a lot of time.

If you rebooted, the only person who could install applications or make system changes is anyone in the Domain Admins group. I like to save myself time and add the user of this PC to the Power Users.

If you don't add it before you reboot from adding the PC to the domain, you have to login as an administrator and give the user Power User or Administrator group rights, then log back out and log back in as the user to install applications.

I am the administrator and this is my laptop, so I am going to add myself to the Administrators group on the local PC. To do this, right click on the My Computer icon in the Start Bar. Choose Manage and you will get the Computer Management screen as shown in figure 4.17.

Click on the Local Users and Groups, then choose Groups, Administrators (Or Power Users) and enter the login ID of the person you want to give the rights to. Now this will not give the person any extra domain rights but it will allow the user control over their own PC.

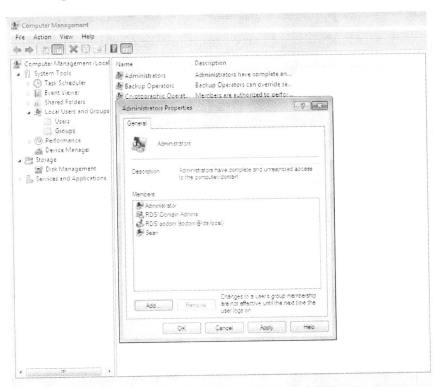

Figure 4.17

You will probably need the domain administrator's login and password one more time to add a domain user to any of the groups. Click Ok, find the restart screen from when you added the PC to the domain and click OK again as shown in figure 4.18.

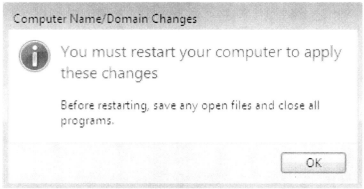

Figure 4.18

Personalization

We will look at personalizing your Windows 7 experience in this chapter. As you can see, you can make changes in the Control Panel, Appearance and Personalization then choose Personalization in figure 4.19.

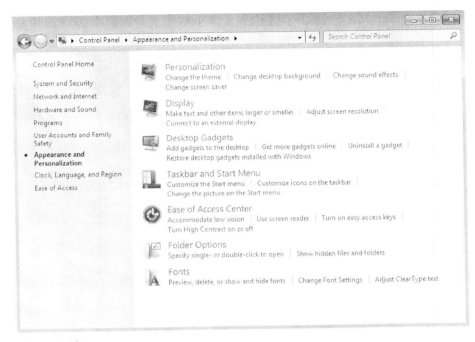

Figure 4.19

In figure 4.20 you see the different options for configuring your desktop, background, colors, sound, and the screen saver.

Setting Backgrounds

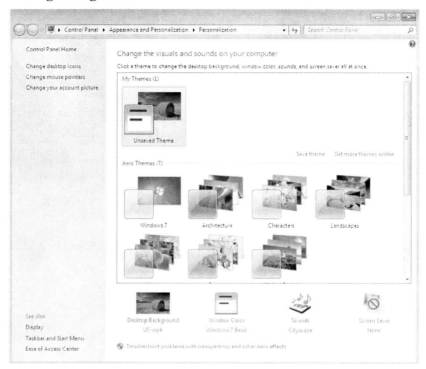

Figure 4.20

You can click on any of the pictures to make them your desktop background or choose your own. In figure 4.21 you will see the Windows colors and appearance options that you can choose instead of a picture for your background.

Setting Colors and Appearance

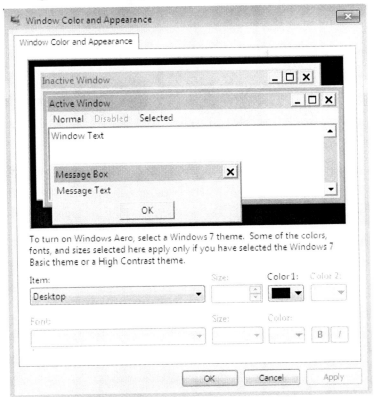

Figure 4.21

Let's say you want to stop the Windows login music, or change your beeps to a dog bark. How would you do that? Well make it a .WAV file and change the sounds until you find one you like, as shown in figure 4.22. You can also choose to use themes you have downloaded or that come preconfigured in Windows 7.

Sound Settings

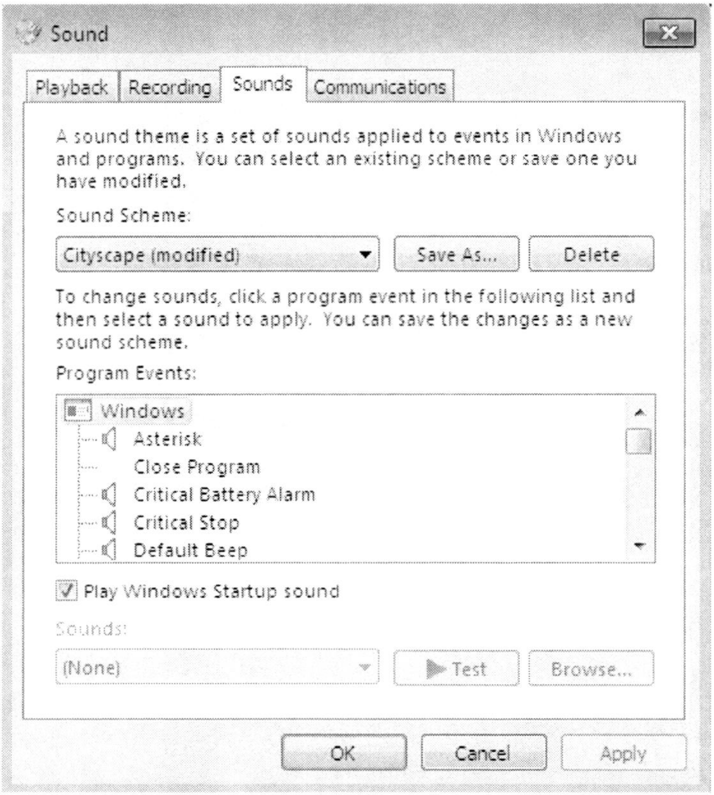

Figure 4.22

Screen savers keep your screens from getting burned in images that you can see as shadows when you are using your computer. These are caused by the same screen burning the pixels from being in too long. In figure 4.23 you will see where you can change the screensaver and the settings.

Configuring Screen Saver Settings

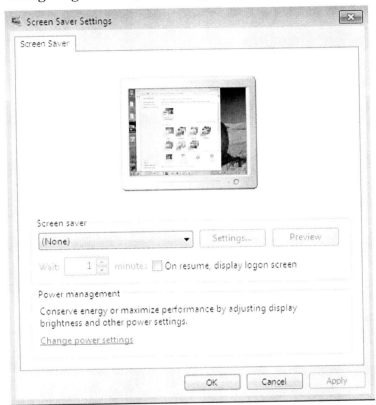

Figure 4.23

Configuring Desktop Icons

Figure 4.24

Many of these icons were on the desktop by default in Windows 98 and Windows 2000. In XP and Vista these icons were there in Classic Mode or by selection. In Windows 7 they are here only by selecting them in this screen. By placing a checkmark as shown in figure 4.24 on any of these boxes the corresponding icon will show up on the desktop.

Changing the Mouse Pointer Properties

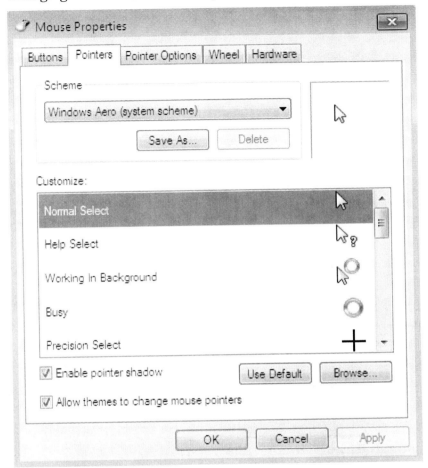

Figure 4.25

The screen shown in figure 4.25, allows you to change the properties of your mouse. This includes customizing the pointer, effects, buttons, sensitivity and much more.

Change Your Profile Picture

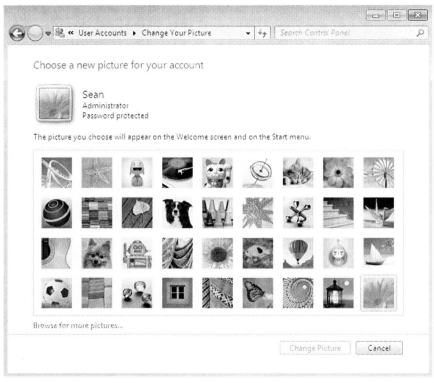

Figure 4.26

This screen shown in figure 4.26 allows you to change your profile picture to any of the preinstalled pictures or to browse for more pictures or search for your own.

Change Your Display Settings

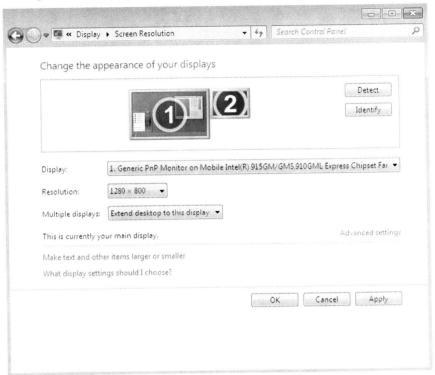

Figure 4.27

The screen in figure 4.27 shows the different options for adjusting your screen size, adding a second monitor, and adjusting the advanced settings. For more information on the advanced setting please see:

http://www.sevenforums.com/tutorials/258-color-bit-depth-display-settings.html

Chapter 5 - Super Bar (Task Bar)

In this book I tend to call the Taskbar, the Start Bar several places as many people can understand what I am talking about. However, many people at Microsoft and on the Internet are referring to Windows 7 version as the "Superbar". So from here on out I will try to refer to it as the Superbar.

In Microsoft texts the Taskbar is still named "Taskbar" in Windows 7. Let's take a look at this new bar in figure 5.1 which you will immediately notice is much glassier look than previous versions of Windows.

Figure 5.1

Like Vista's task bar, the Windows 7 taskbar also provides a preview of the running applications by using their running icons by default. Also there is a small sliver bar next to each icon which allows you to view multiple instances of that application. So if you have two word documents open you can view and then select the one you want to see as shown in figure 5.2.

Figure 5.2

In the rest of this chapter I am going to walk you through customizing the Superbar, the Superbar options, the features of the Superbar, and some Group Policy Edits.

Customizing the Superbar Properties

If we right click on the round Windows 7 logo or the Superbar we get two and select Properties you will see the options in figure 5.3. We will then select the Toolbar Tab to add some additional features to our Superbar. In figure 5.3 you will see I have right clicked on the Superbar and chosen Properties. In the Toolbars Tab I have checked the Address tab and clicked Apply. In figure 5.4 you will see the changes this has made to the Superbar.

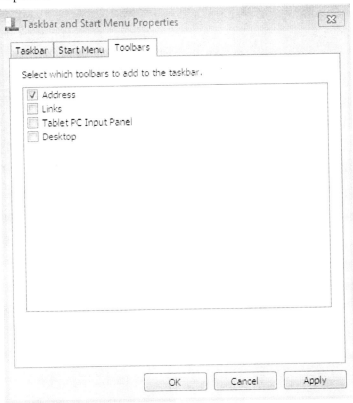

Figure 5.3

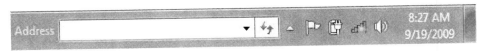

Figure 5.4

Next, I will check the Link option and press apply. In Figure 5.5 you will see the Link option on the Superbar to the left and the menu that appears when you get when you click the Link option.

Figure 5.5

The next option is for those who use Windows 7 on a Tablet PC. But if you have a but don't use a Tablet PC, it is fun to use your mouse or a graphics tablet to play with it and try and convert what you write to actual typed text. In figure 5.6 you will see I have now checked the Tablet PC option and pressed apply. I have then clicked on the new option on the bar which brings up the Tablet PC menu box.

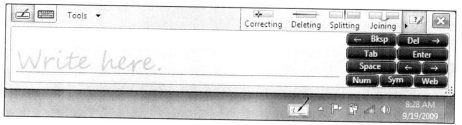

Figure 5.6

106

The last option is the Desktop option which places all your shortcuts and folders from your desktop onto the menu. An arrow to the left gives you the additional files or folders which are contained on the desktop. Also the folders contained in your Documents folder are also listed. Also you have shortcuts to My Computer, the Network, and the Control Panel all accessible in one easy place as shown in figure 5.7.

Figure 5.7

Show Desktop Button

This is one of my favorite icons in the taskbar. It has got a slightly different location in the new Superbar right next to the clock. This new feature is different from the old Desktop Icon which minimized all your open application windows. If you had 8 windows open, you had to click each one to maximize them again after pressing the old Desktop Icon.

This new button as shown in figure 5.8 minimizes all of your open application windows which are maximized on the screen. When you are done looking at your desktop, simply click the button again and walla, all of your windows are back open just the way they were before.

Figure 5.8

Using the Superbar Customize Feature

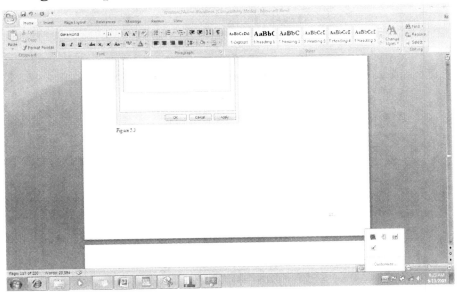

Figure 5.9

In figure 5.9 above you will notice the little up arrow on the Superbar by the clock. You can also see that I have clicked on this arrow and it has given me options. There are other shortcuts at the top which are Superbar icons I do not want to see on the Superbar. But let's say I did want to see them all or one or more of these on the Superbar. I would click the Customize option.

In figure 5.10, you will see each Icon I have available and a drop down menu next to each of them giving you three options. These options are:

- Show icon and notifications
- Hide icon and notifications
- Only Show notifications

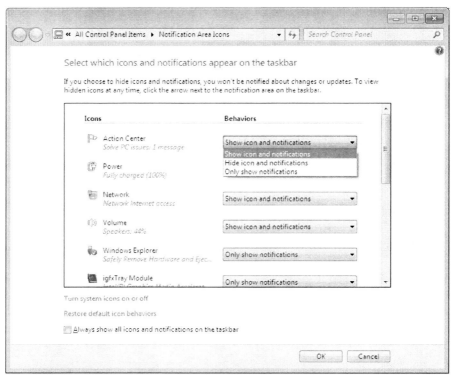

Figure 5.10

If I want to see all of the Icons on the menu bar I would simply click on
Always show all icons and notifications on the taskbar and click OK as
shown on figure 5.11. You will notice the changes on the Superbar where
it now shows all the icons.

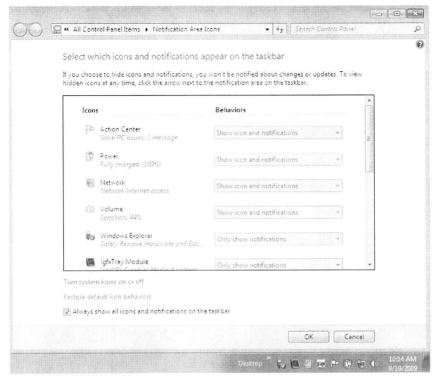

Figure 5.11

Windows Aero Overview

Aero is a new feature introduced in Windows Vista and expanded in Windows 7 to improve the desktop look and experience. Aero requires a display adapter compatible with Windows Display Driver Model (WDDM) and a Windows 7 Windows Experience Index of 3.0 or better to work. We will talk about how to view these options later in this section.

First though let's get a look at the items we will focus on in this section which are:

- **Aero Glass**

- **Aero Peek**

- **Aero Snap**

- **Aero Shake**

- **Windows Flip 3D**

In most circumstance, if the PC's display card satisfies the minimum requirement to run Windows Aero, which appears to be not much different, to what's required in Windows Vista:

1. 1 GHz 32-bit (x86) or 64-bit (x64) processor

2. 1 GB (gigabyte) of RAM memory

3. DirectX 9 compatible GPU with a minimum of 128 MB of Video RAM

4. Windows Display Driver Model (WDDM) driver

5. Windows 7 will automatically enable Windows Aero upon installation.

> **Alert:** *Aero is not a feature of Windows 7 Starter Edition.*

Sometimes Windows Aero may not be turned on, or is having problem to enable. This is for many reasons such unsupported video drivers, outdated or unsupported VGA graphic display card, not meeting the above requirements, or Windows 7 just does not automatically enable. Let's take a look at how to find out what is wrong and see if we can get Windows 7 to enable this feature with the instructions in the next section.

How to Enable Aero in Windows 7

1. Once you have finished Installing Windows 7 install updated video drivers for your windows 7.

2. Refresh your WEI (Windows Experience Index) Score. In order to refresh WEI right on My Computer -> Properties, A New window with System information will be displayed as shown in figure 5.12.

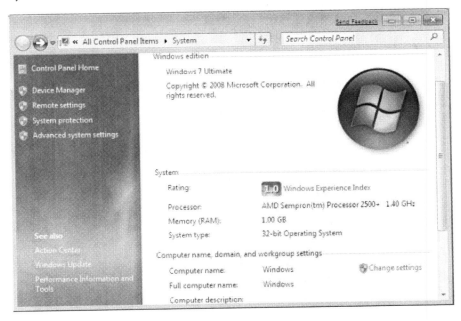

Figure 5.12

3. Click on Performance Information and Tools at the bottom right side of window and view your PC's WEI Score as shown in figure 5.13. A score of 3.0 or better is required for Windows 7 to automatically enable this feature.

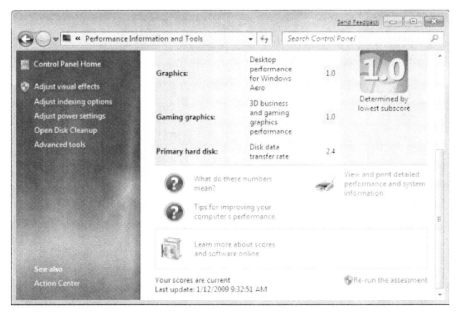

Figure 5.13

4. Now click Re-run the assessment

(Or you can simply Click on start->type **cmd** and type following command: **winsat formal)**

Once your Windows Experience Index is recalculated and if it's higher then 3.0, Aero in Windows 7 will Aero Glass will automatically be enabled.

> **NOTE:** You *can change colors by right clicking on desktop-> Personalize -> Select Windows Colors.*

Aero Peek Feature

Aero Peak is the new and improved thumbnail previews added to the Superbar. This is very important when you want to switch between applications when you have multiple windows open. You might need to minimize every other window opened to look for your application. You can also use ALT + TAB or use Windows Flip 3D to browse the applications.

With the new Superbar, you can just hover on the thumbnail previews to get a preview of that window while the other windows fade away into glass sheets and easily switch to your application!

Aero Snap Feature

There is also a really cool feature which allows you to drag an application to the left or right until the screen dims as shown in figure 5.14. When you release, your application will be exactly half the screen width.

Figure 5.14

Note: *The Windows Key + the right arrow key will produce the same result.*

It's a great way of comparing documents side by side as shown in figure 5.15.

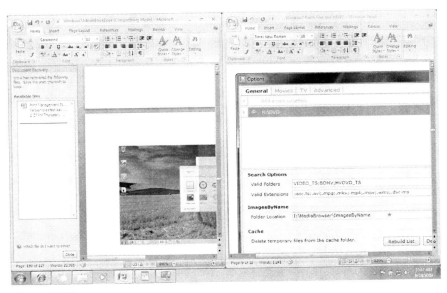

Figure 5.15

Aero Shake Feature

Aero Shake is a new feature to help wear out your mouse quicker so that manufacturers of mice can start upping their sales counts. I am just kidding. What Aero Shake does is allows you to shake an application on your desktop by clicking at the top and moving quickly left and right. By doing this all the other windows you have opened except for the one you are moving left and right will quickly minimize.

It's a nice feature that I can see some practical use for, but I think they need to work on the sensitivity so users don't wear out their mice. Of course it does have some exercise value. Maybe they should call it the "Microsoft Fit" function. I mean Wii came out with their version.

Aero Glass Feature

Aero Glass effect is one of new features of Windows Vista and is now extended to Windows 7. It features a translucent glass design with sublet windows animations and new windows colors.

The Aero Glass effects all of your open application windows makes them transparent like glass as shown below in figure 5.16.

Figure 5.16

Windows Flip 3D

Windows Flip improves on the ALT+TAB method for flipping between application windows; while Windows Flip 3D dynamically displays all open windows in a graceful three-dimensional view as shown in figure 5.17 which shows the results of hovering over the Internet Explorer icon on the Superbar.

Windows Flip 3D uses the dimension of visual depth to give you a more comprehensive view of your open windows, helping you sidestep chaos even as you juggle myriad open files and programs.

Windows Flip 3D can even render images of live processes such as currently playing video. Use the START+TAB keys to initiate the 3-D view, then flip through open windows by using arrow keys or the scroll wheel on your mouse to quickly identify and select the one you want. Navigating your desktop has never been this fun.

Figure 5.17

120

Troubleshooting Windows Aero

Whatever the cause of your Windows Aero failure, there is the easy way to fix all issues, bugs or problems related to Windows Aero, and then turn on and enable the Windows Aero feature in Windows 7. We discussed a way up in the Windows Aero Overview but thanks to a new troubleshooting task tool added in Windows 7 even easier.

To troubleshoot Aero effects such as transparency in Windows 7, follow these steps:

1. Make sure that **Windows Experience Index** has been calculated and computed.

2. Click on **Start** menu.

3. Type the following text into the Start Search box:

   Aero

4. Click on the search result listing under Control Panel group named, "Find and fix problems with transparency and other visual effects". Right click and choose Open. The result is displayed in figure 5.18.

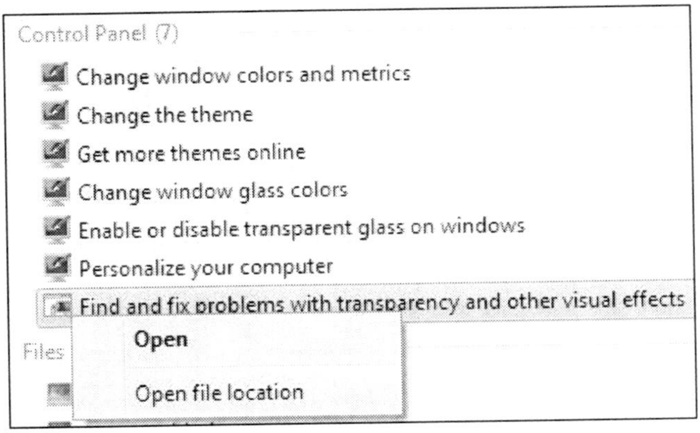

Figure 5.18

Note: *If you don't see "Find and fix problems with transparency and other visual effects" in the search results, click on Control Panel option displayed in the results to see all Aero related.*

5. Next an "Aero – Troubleshooting Computer Problems" wizard will appear. Click on **Next** button. As shown in figure 5.19. After clicking Next you will see the screen shown in figure 5.20.

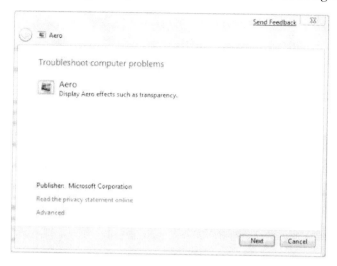

Figure 5.19

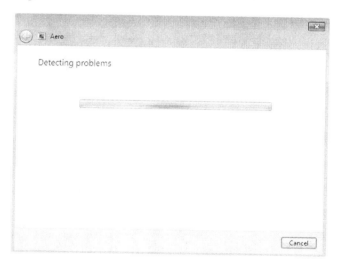

Figure 5.20

6. The troubleshooting wizard will attempt to detect any problems by running a series of checks as shown in figure 5.21.

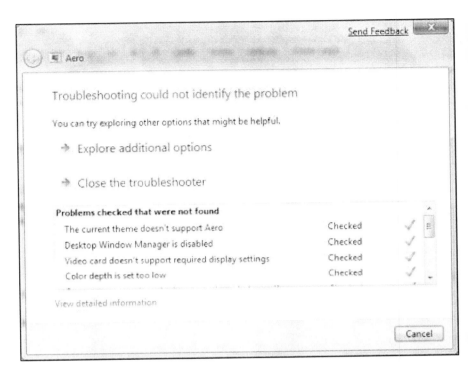

Figure 5.21

Alert: *Items with a red cross which indicates a problem which may prevent Aero from working properly, fix the issues and then rerun the "Find and fix problems with transparency and other visual effects" troubleshooting wizard again.*

Note: *There are also other registry hacks available on the Internet to force Aero to work as long as your display card supports WDDI. I actually created a whole chapter on these hacks but the Editor of this book, as well as the Technical Editor voiced concerns about it. So it got removed. But you can Bing or Google, "Aero Hacks" and you will find them. Also note though, that if you do something to screw up your PC by using these hacks, Microsoft will most likely not help you fix it.*

Other Superbar Features and Customizations

In this section let's talk about some other cool features and customizations that can be made to the Superbar. We will take a look at the following items:

- Group Policy Editor customizations
- Identifying open and closed applications
- Application progress bars
- Application Previews
- Pin and unpin applications to the Superbar
- Customizing the Superbar With The Taskbar Properties Taskbar Tab

Group Policy0

.-+

Z7 Editor Customizations

There are a number of customizations that can be made to the Superbar from the Group Policy Editor. So many in fact that I realized I could write an entire book just on this subject. So I am going to show you how to turn off the taskbar thumbnails on the Superbar. Then on your own you can scroll through the different items you can modify until your heart is content. I counted 355 options under the Start Menu. It might be more or less depending on your Windows 7 version.

So how you enable or disable thumbnail previews in Windows 7 is follow these instructions:

> 1. Click on start and type on search bar **gpedit.msc** and press enter
>
> 2. Now navigate to **User Configuration, Administrative Templates**, and **Start Menu and Taskbar** in left window of the Group Policy Editor as shown in figure 5.22. You will notice in the right window all of the options I talked about before.

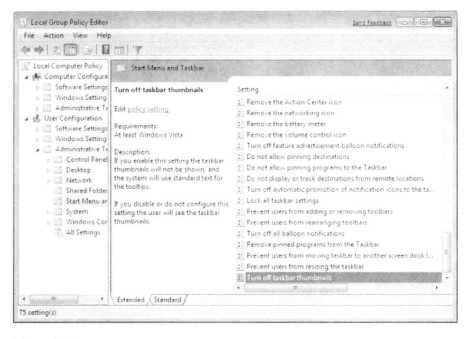

Figure 5.22

3. Locate **"Turn off Taskbar Thumbnails"** in right window of the Group policy editor and double click on it.

4. Select Disable and then click apply as shown in figure 5.23.

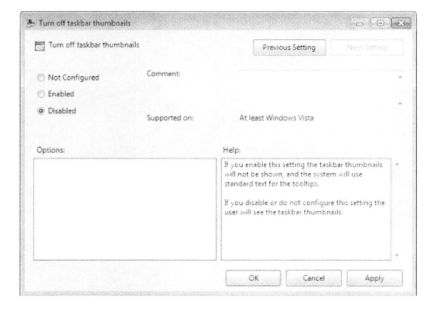

Figure 5.23

5. Now check your Taskbar. You should now show just the file names instead of pictures.

Application Progress Bars

The application progress bars for downloading from the Internet or saving applications is actually a new unique feature. As shown below in figure 5.24, you will see Internet Explorer downloading a PDF and a search that I have running. The search is at 36% and the download is at 48%. I need to note that only some applications provide progress bars. Not all.

Figure 5.24

One item that became apparent to me is that when I had multiple instances of downloads in Internet Explorer it becomes difficult to keep track of multiple progresses in the same application. If you hover your mouse over the applications Icon on the Superbar however, you can get a more accurate look at where the progress is on each individual

Pin and Unpin Applications to the Superbar

Unlike earlier versions of Windows you can now very easy go to Pin and Unpin icons to the Superbar. This is a way to keep your most used application shortcuts right on the Superbar . The Pin to Taskbar is available if you right click and application in the Start menu, Programs menu, or right off an open application already in the Superbar. In figure 5.25, I am pinning Microsoft Word to the Superbar using the Pin to Taskbar option. You will note I can also choose to pin the application to the Start Menu where I am getting the Windows Word shortcut from.

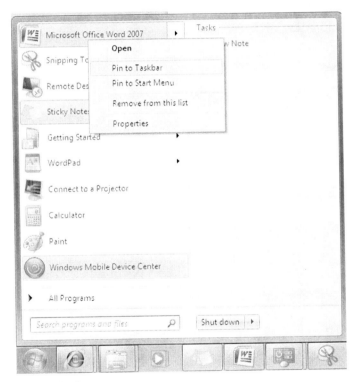

Figure 5.25

Now that it is pinned to the Superbar anytime I log out or restart the computer the Microsoft Word shortcut and icon will be displayed in the Superbar. If I right click on the Microsoft Word icon in the Superbar I will have the option of Unpinning the program as shown in figure 5.26.

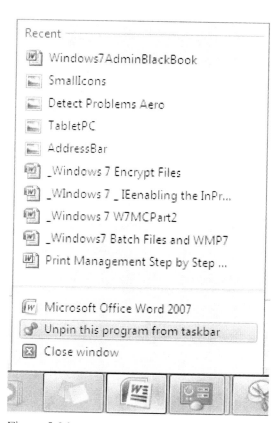

Figure 5.26

Customizing the Superbar with the Taskbar and Start Menu Properties Taskbar Tab

Occasionally, some users might not like the new way of grouping items, especially the icon overlay display where sometimes it becomes difficult for some users to identify which applications are running and closed.

You can easily access these options in the Taskbar properties dialog window as shown in Figure 5.27.

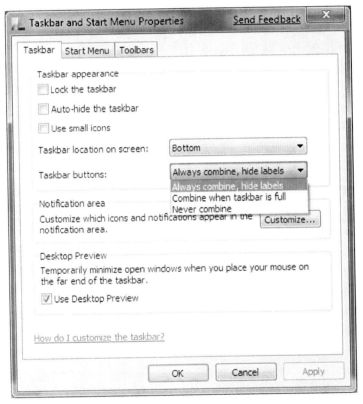

Figure 5.27

Below are screenshots of taskbar buttons with different options as shown in figures 5.28, 5.29, and 5.30.:

1) Always combine, hide labels (default behavior)

Figure 5.28

2) Combine when taskbar is full (similar to earlier versions of Windows)

Figure 5.29

3) Using small icons

Figure 5.30

The Superbar is indeed a major feature update for Windows 7. Of course, many users will find the Superbar initially surprising as it needs some time to grasp the new features, but once you become familiar with the Superbar, you will start enjoying the simplicity of the new evolved Windows Taskbar.

Chapter 6 – File Security and Encryption

Windows 7 is full of ways to protect yourself when you are using your computer. There are so many threats out there that it is important to be proactive and educated on possible threats to your computer and do what you can to detect and prevent them.

In this section we will show you how to keep applications off your network PC's, how to encrypt your sensitive data, and how to protect your privacy when using Windows Media Player included with your Windows 7 operating system.

AppLocker

AppLocker as shown in figure 6.1, it is a new application control feature available in Microsoft Windows 7 that helps eliminate unwanted and unknown applications within an organization's network to providing a much more productive and secure environment.

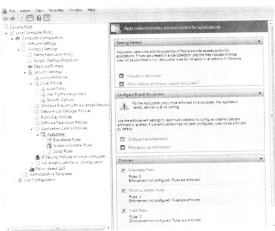

Figure 6.1

These screens are blown up in the next few pages so don't go grab your magnifying glass just yet.

AppLocker answers the need for application control with a simple and flexible application that allows administrators to specify exactly what is allowed to run on the computer in their network environment. There are many benefits to using AppLocker in your network such as:

- Stop unlicensed software from being installed or run in your environment.
- Preventing vulnerable, unauthorized applications from being installed or run in your environment.
- Prevent user from running applications which waste time.
- Stopping users from running applications that needlessly consume network bandwidth.
- Preventing users from running applications that possible contain viruses or malware.
- Allow users to install and run software and updates based upon their business needs
- Ensure compliance of corporate policies and industry regulations for PCI DSS, Sarbanes-Oxley, HIPAA, Basel II, and state identity theft protection acts.
- Reduce the cost of repair for users who install software which causes their PC to have issues or infects other devices in the network.

AppLocker provides a powerful solution using three rule types: allow, deny, and exception. Allow rules limit execution of applications to a "good list" of programs and applications. Deny rules take the opposite approach and disallow all programs and applications on the "bad list". Exception rules allow you to exclude files from an allow/deny rule that would normally be included such as a rule to "allow everything in the Windows Operating System to run, except the built-in games."

AppLocker is configured in the Group Policy Editor in Local Computer Policy, Security Settings, Application Control Policies, and then AppLocker as shown in figure 6.2. In figure 6.3 you will see the options that you can configure for AppLocker.

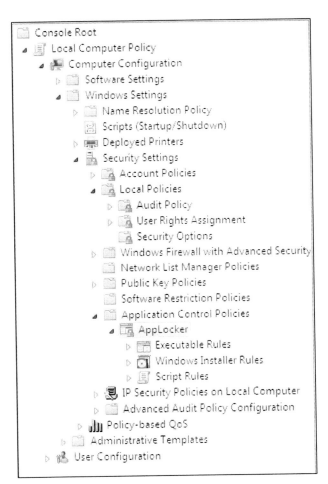

Figure 6.2

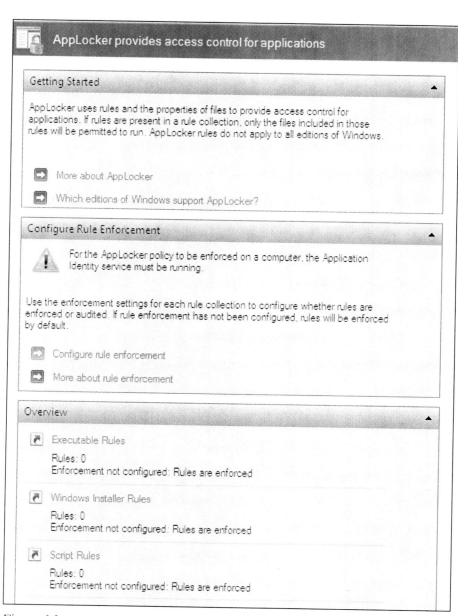

Figure 6.3

136

User Access Control (UAC)

To access UAC settings click the Start button, type *UAC*, and click on Change User Account Control Settings. This page is relatively simple with only four options to decide the level of security you want associated with your profile. These options range from never notify to always notify.

Figures 6.4, 6.5, 6.6, and 6.7 show the four options available and when you will receive an alert. The default is shown in figure 6.4.

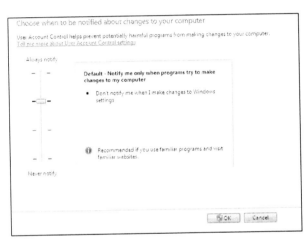

Figure 6.4

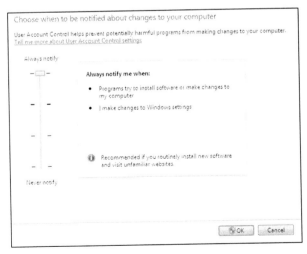

Figure 6.5

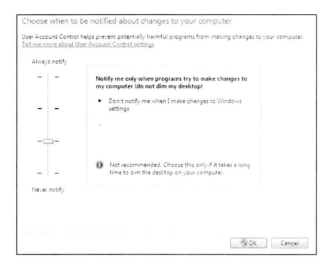

Figure 6.6

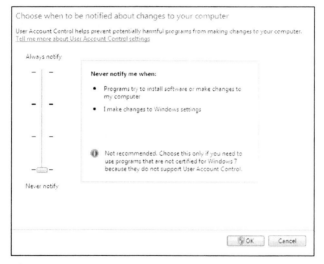

Figure 6.7

138

BitLocker

BitLocker Drive Encryption is a new feature that provides protection for operating hard drives, external drives, and removable data drives in case they are lost or stolen. BitLocker is a way of encrypting the data on drives and requiring authentication to access the information.

BitLocker encrypts your drives so others cannot access them without a password. BitLocker comes in two flavors in Windows 7 which are BitLocker and BitLock To Go.

You can also force the PC to book from an encryption key on a USB flash drive. You can insert the USB flash drive into the computer during startup to allow it to book. The USB flash drive is used to unlock the computer.

When enabling BitLocker on a hard drive or removable drives, BitLocker can use the following unlock methods:

Password: You can use a password to unlock your BitLocker encrypted data drives and Group Policy settings can be used to set minimum password lengths.

Smart card: BitLocker allows you to use a compatible certificate on your smart card. By default, BitLocker will choose the certificate unless you have multiple compatible certificates, in which case you must choose the certificate to use.

BitLocker To Go was specially created to encrypt the data on your portable media. With an increasing number of key drives being used, the loss of sensitive data is becoming more of a threat.

Encrypting Your Thumb Drive

To encrypt your thumb drive, do the following you should plug your thumb drive into a USB port, click the Start button, type BitLocker, and click on BitLocker Drive Encryption. Next to your drive letter of your thumb drive, click Turn on BitLocker as shown in figure 6.8.

Choose a password and click Continue as shown in figure 6.9. You will be given the option to save your recovery key (used if you forget your password) or print it. If you save the file, ensure the file is stored somewhere safe and then click Next as shown in figure 6.10.

You will then need to confirm your chosen settings, the password and click Start Encrypting as shown in figure 6.11.

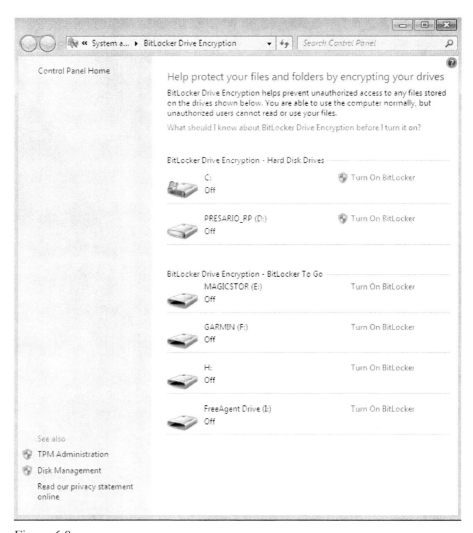

Figure 6.8

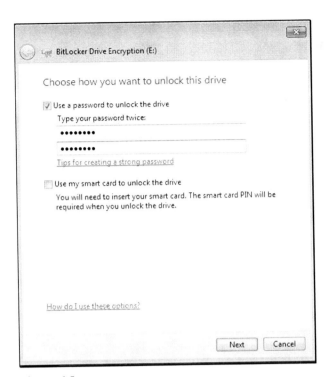

Figure 6.9

Figure 6.10

Figure 6.11

After you click Start Encrypting you will see the screen in figure 6.12. Please notice the figure above where it warns that large drives may take quite a while.

Figure 6.12

Now that I am done, I am going to try and access the drive I just encrypted. As soon as I try a new screen appears asking me to enter a password before I can access the drive as shown in figure 6.13.

142

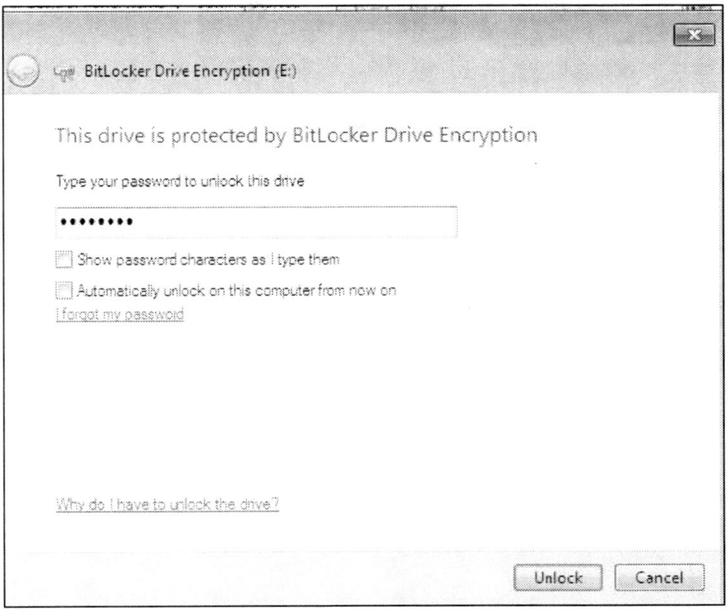
BitLocker Drive Encryption (E:)
This drive is protected by BitLocker Drive Encryption
Type your password to unlock this drive
Show password characters as I type them
Automatically unlock on this computer from now on
I forgot my password
Why do I have to unlock the drive?
Unlock
Cancel

Figure 6.13

Setting up Your HomeGroup

HomeGroup is a new feature in Windows 7 that makes it easy to share your libraries and printers on a home network. Homegroup provides password protection and a choice of what you want to share with others.

A Homegroup is created in the Control Panel under the Network and Internet as shown in figure 6.14.

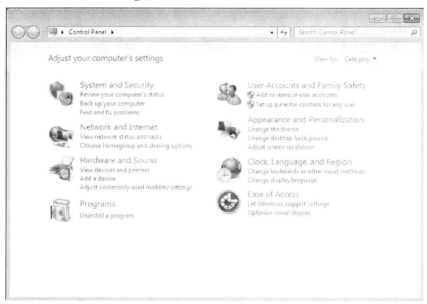

Figure 6.14

You will see the options for the Network and Internet settings as shown in figure 6.15. The second option called Homegroup is where you create or remove a Homegroup or make changes to the settings.

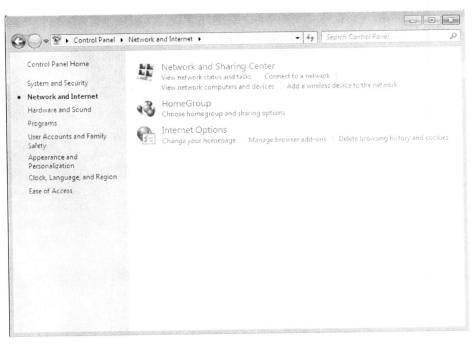

Figure 6.15

If no Homegroup is configured, the first screen you will see is the one pictured in figure 6.16.

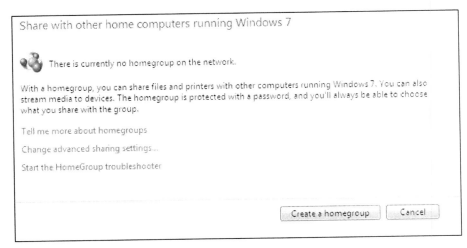

Figure 6.16

Once you select Create a Homegroup, the next screen as shown in figure 6.17 allows you to decide which items you will be sharing with others by clicking the box and placing a checkmark next to the option. Choose from Pictures, Documents, Printers, Music, and Videos.

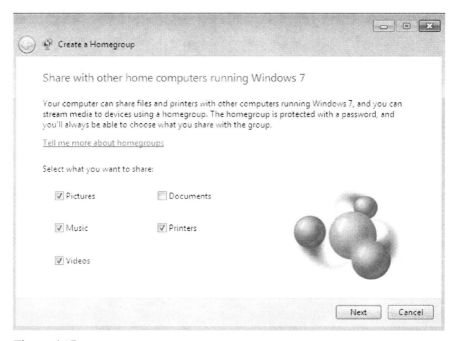

Figure 6.17

Next, Windows will automatically prepare your HomeGroup for you. Once this part is done, you will need to get a shared password, which allows other computers, running Windows 7, to connect to your HomeGroup. Figure 6.18 shows the screen where you are given your password.

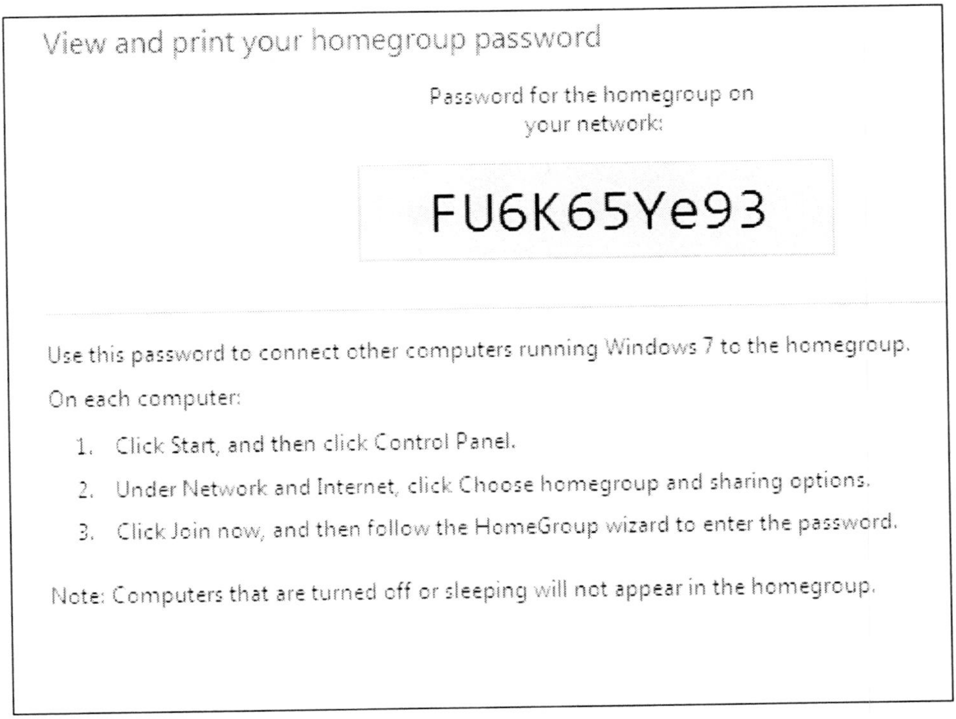

View and print your homegroup password

Password for the homegroup on
your network:

FU6K65Ye93

Use this password to connect other computers running Windows 7 to the homegroup.

On each computer:

1. Click Start, and then click Control Panel.

2. Under Network and Internet, click Choose homegroup and sharing options.

3. Click Join now, and then follow the HomeGroup wizard to enter the password.

Note: Computers that are turned off or sleeping will not appear in the homegroup.

Figure 6.18

The password is also available to view whenever you need by going back to the Homegroup link in Network and Sharing as shown in figure 6.19.

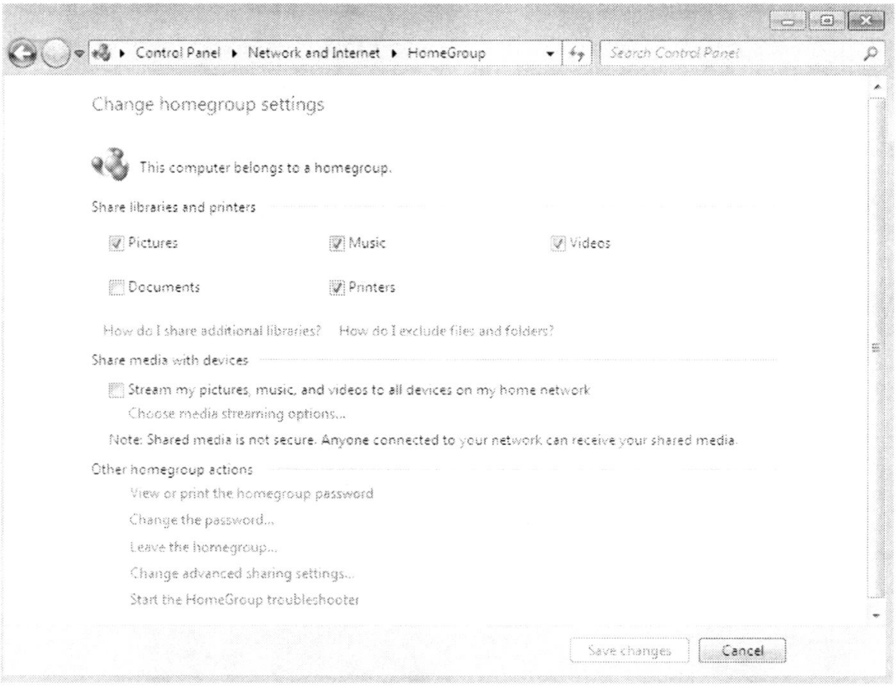

Figure 6.19

Note: *Joining a Homegroup is easy. To join your current HomeGroup, go to your second PC and connect to the same network (wireless or wired) the HomeGroup is configured on. You will automatically be prompted to join the HomeGroup. Click "Join Now" and type in your HomeGroup password.*

Chapter 7 – Maintaining Windows 7

In a perfect world your computer would never break, never need maintenance, never slow down, never get a virus, and never lose any of your data. Well this computer you have and the operating system are very technical and they have a lot of moving parts. Not to mention the environment you place it in can be just as bad as anything else. One of my customers has about 20 employees, but he runs a machine shop and my technicians are out there every other week performing maintenance on the PC's and they still break down. Also just using your PC, moving files, doing searches, and just about anything you do with your PC creates a need for regular maintenance.

If there wasn't a need to fix and maintain Windows PC's and servers, there wouldn't be a platoon of certified people out there to work on them. You would take the PC out of the box, it would be ready to go and you would never have a need to call technical support, or fix anything. It would be a perfect world. Well it's not so you better continue reading this chapter.

Let's take a look at what we will cover in this chapter some more features of the Action Center such as:

- Windows Update

- Windows Defragmenter

- Windows Disk Cleanup

- Windows Check Disk (CHKDSK)

- Windows Backup

- Advanced Boot Options

Note: *Regardless of the version of Windows 7 you have purchased. All the features in this chapter are in included.*

System Security with Windows Updates

To get bugs in the operating system fixed automatically, stay safe on a network and the Internet you need to keep your system up to date. In this day and age it is absolutely essential step in maintaining a secure computer environment. When threats emerge, Windows has been quick to patch and make changes to their operating system to quickly fix the issue. This has been thanks to the Windows Update program which has been completely redesigned in Windows 7. The Windows Update setting page available in the Windows Action Center allows you to configure your Windows Update settings as shown in figure 7.1.

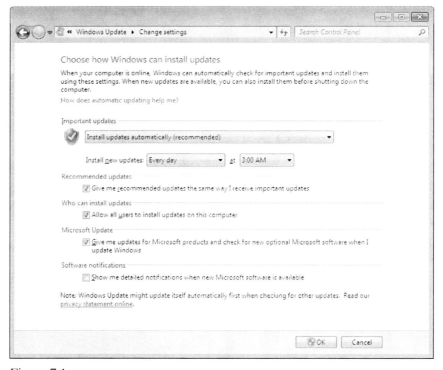

Figure 7.1

Microsoft routinely releases security updates on the second Tuesday of each month on what s known as, "Patch Tuesday". Most other Microsoft updates are when the need arises, such as when a fix is developed for a newly discovered problem. If you keep the settings at the default setting, updates will install automatically.

The Change Settings dialog box lets you specify how you want Windows Updates to operate. The options allow you to specify whether to download and let you specify which ones to install, specify which updates to install and then download, or just disable Windows Updates all together as shown in figure 7.2.

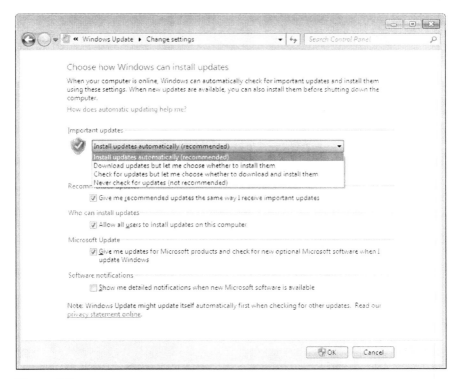

Figure 7.2

If you use the Install Updates Automatically (Recommended) option Windows will come out of sleep mode automatically at the time you selected and update your system. If you have either the "download, but don't install" or "check, but don't download or install" options selected, Windows Update notifies you with a flag notification when new updates are available for you to approve. This is very time consuming and not recommended.

"Who Can Install Updates", allows an administrator of the PC to either allow all users to install updates or uncheck the box to allow only administrators to install updates.

"Microsoft Update", if checked allows you to update for other Microsoft products other than the operating system and also install software that Microsoft recommends.

"Software Notifications", this gives you detailed information of the updates Microsoft has installed. If you have ever gone to Microsoft's update website and installed updates you see a reason, what the update does for you and the Microsoft identification code.

> **Alert:** *If Windows Updates fails to download and install an error code will appear in a notification message on the flag on your Superbar. It will also display a link to get help about the possible problem. If Windows Updates fail you will want to find out why right away. It could be an indication of a bigger problem such as a virus, worm, Trojan, or malware.*

Sidebar: What if an update gives me trouble?

If you suspect a particular update creates a problem, some updates can be removed. To see if an update can be removed, look under Windows Update, click Installed Updates in the left window. This will take you to Control Panel, Programs. You will be able to see the installed updates.

Those which are not security updates and can be uninstalled will give you the option to uninstall. The page only lists updates that can be uninstalled. To see all updates that have been installed whether they are removable or not go to Windows Update and click View Update History.

Defragmenting Disks

When your system is a new system it is really fast and the computers processor has plenty of RAM, and when it runs out it has nice speedy hard drive space to act a virtual memory. What can happen if you don't maintain your hard disk?

What is fragmentation anyway?

When you first get your computer there is plenty of space to put your files anywhere and in a nice, easy to find space all together on the hard drive. But as you go along, the drive starts having a hard time trying to find enough space in between the little files it's placed for the bigger ones it is now placing on the drive. So the operating system starts splitting up the files and placing them all over the hard drive in pieces. After a while there are so many split up files that it slows the PC down looking for the files so it can piece them all back together and show you that nice 200MB PDF you want to see so bad. It doesn't seem like much until you know that on an NTFS volume larger than 2 GB in size, the cluster size is 4 KB. So if you have 400MB movie it is over 100,000 fragmented pieces.

After a while hard disk performance becomes a bottleneck and everyday your operation of the PC starts to slow things down. It starts with being noticed when you play movies, video clips, and perform DVD-burning. A little while longer your hard drive becomes slow even opening a small Word document or going to the Internet.

That is where Windows Defragmenter becomes your friend. I recommend you defrag your hard disks weekly. I you do, it should only take about 10 to 20 minutes and your hard drive will always stay healthy in terms of fragmentation. The longer you wait, the longer it takes to defragment the hard disks. I was called to a customer that had slowness at a cement plant recently. The PC was 4 years old and probably has never been defragmented. It took the PC about 2 days to perform this simple routine. Imagine all the frustration and lost productivity she had because of the lack of knowledge of this small simple process.

Windows Defragmenter has been in every version of Windows. In Windows 7 it is improved. Unlike previous versions Disk Defragmenter allows you to configure it to run as a low-priority background task once a week. If you set it run in the middle of the night, unless you are a night owl, you can set it and forget it. Let it run on its own.

Figure 7.3 shows Windows Defragmenter by going to Start, All Programs, Accessories, System Tools, and the Disk Defragmenter.

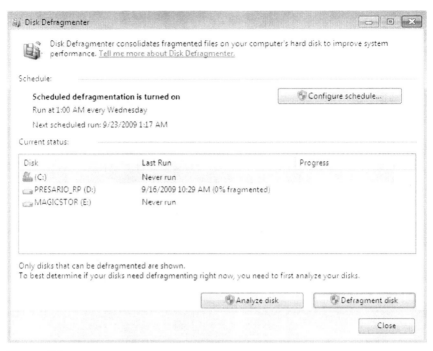

Figure 7.3

To configure Windows Disk Defragmenter to run on its own click the, "Configure Schedule...", button and the scheduler window will appear as shown in figure 7.4.

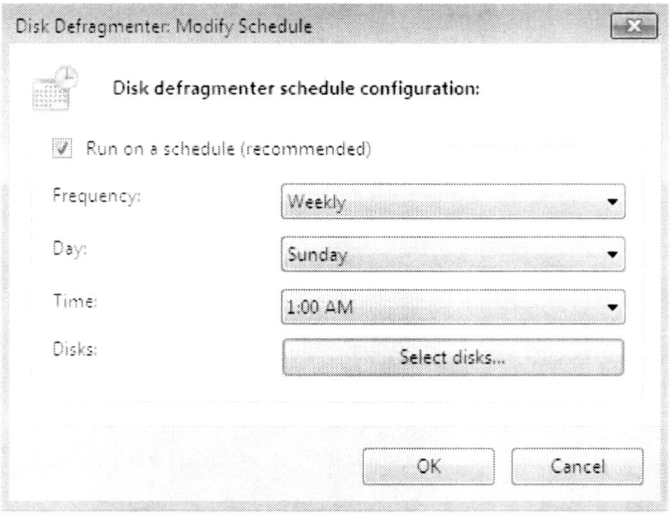

Figure 7.4

Pick a day of the week, the time and then select the disk you would like this to run on as shown in figure 7.5.

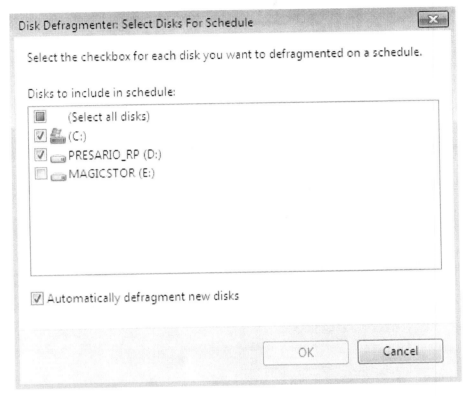

Figure 7.5

Selecting the, "Automatically defragment new disks" will auto add any drives which are connected whether they are large USB or even thumb drives. So it truly is a set it and forget it utility.

Running Disk Defragmenter

Disk Defragmenter allows you to run additional options from the command line. To use disk defragmenter from the command line, type "cmd" at the Windows Programs Bar Search for Files and Programs box. This brings up a Command Prompt window. Next type defrag followed by the drive letter. For instance if you wanted to defrag drive c: you would type "defrag d:" followed by any options you want. To see all of Windows Defragmenters options, type defrag /? at the command prompt.

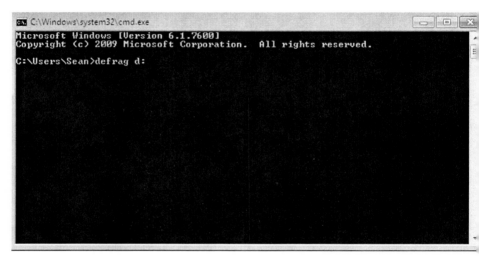

Let's take a look at the options available for the defrag command:

–c   This option defragments all volumes on the computer; use this switch without specifying a specific drive letter or mount point.

–a   This option analyzes the specified volume and displays a summary of the analysis report.

-f   This option consolidates the free space on the specified volume, reducing the chance that large new files will be fragmented.

/r   This option defragments multiple volumes in parallel. If your volumes are on physically separate disks, you might save a bit of time by using this switch.

-v   This option displays complete (verbose) reports. When it used in combination with –a, this switch displays only the analysis report. When used alone, it displays both the analysis and defragmentation reports.

156

−w   This option performs a full defragmentation by consolidating all file fragments, regardless of size.

−b   This option defragments only boot files and applications while leaving the rest of the drive undisturbed.

Note: *There is third party defragmenting software that can be used when Windows Defrag is not enough.*

Alert: *The Disk Defragmenter run from the command prompt does not provide any progress bar. Just a blinking cursor is shown. You can click the Command Prompt window and press CTRL+C to stop the process..*

Windows Check Disk (CHKDSK) and (CHKNTFS)

Along with Defragmenting, your hard disk can get errors as well. If these errors are not me operating system it will continue to place data on these areas. If the data is from these bad areas are not moved from these bad areas of the disk your computer can become unstable and even have what we call a crash. Windows Check Disk can automatically fix disk or file system errors or just look for them and report it to you. It comes in two flavors. One for NTFS drives called chkntfs and one for FAT and FAT32 drives called chkdsk. Let's take a look at both in the next two sections.

CHKDSK

Technically speaking, chkdsk is a DOS utility as shown in figure 7.6 with the different syntaxes and options you can use. It also has a nice GUI with basic controls that you can run by right clicking a drive letter in Computer, right click the drive letter you want to scan, choose Properties, Error-checking, and then Check Now as shown in figure 7.7 and 7.8.

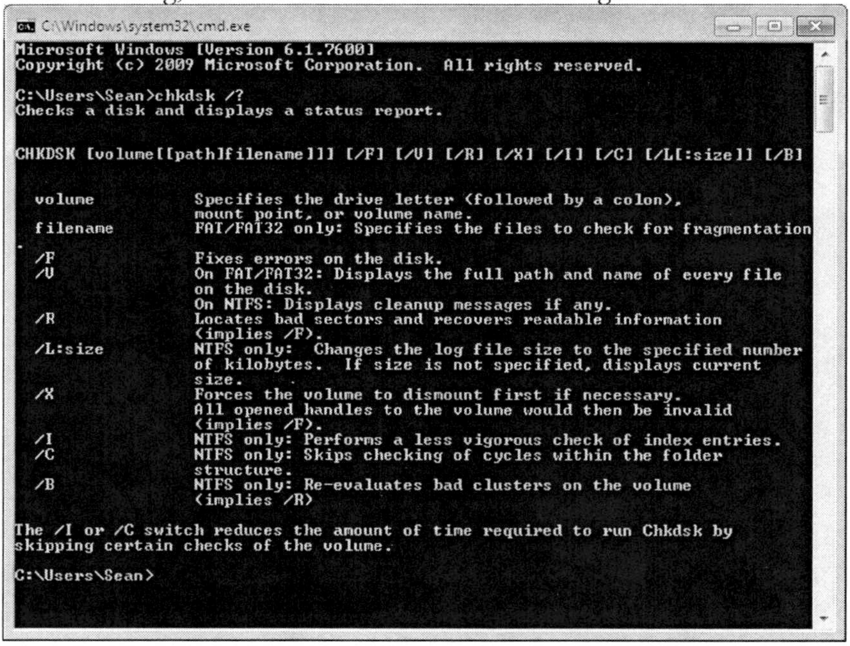

Figure 7.6

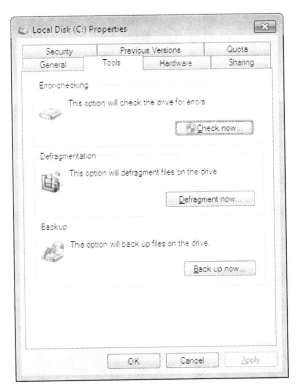

Figure 7.7

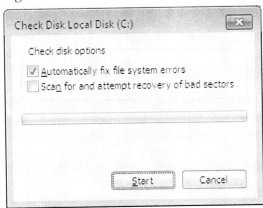

Figure 7.8

By default you have the "Automatically fix file system errors", which is the equivalent of running the chkdsk command in DOS with the /F syntax.

If you check the "Scan For And Attempt Recovery Of Bad Sectors an exhaustive check of the entire disk to find bad sectors and recover readable information stored in those defective location will be run on the hard disk. (Usually requiring a reboot to perform this feature on the next start up.) This option is the equivalent of running the chkdsk command in ODS with the /R syntax.

> **Note:** *Unchecking both boxes simply gives you a report of file system errors without making any changes or error corrections and is the only option which usually does not require a reboot to perform.*

When a reboot is required for the disk checking, the disk check occurs at the beginning of the startup sequence. When your computer starts, a Windows screen notifying you that it's about to perform a scheduled disk check. If you want to delay this check, you have 10 seconds to cancel the operation by pressing the space bar and boot normally in to Windows 7.

If you allow the check to continue, after Check Disk is completed you will get an on screen report of the findings. If the check finds that there are no errors, you see a Disk Check Complete dialog box.

> **Note:** *If Check Disk finds any errors, it puts an entry message in the System Event Log and displays a dialog box listing the errors it found and the repairs it made.*

These are the typical uses of chkdsk for a user. There are other options a shown in 7.6 which are identical in chkntfs and we will explain those further in the next section.

CHKNTFS

Check disk has its own utility errors for drives formatted with NTFS called chkntfs. It is used to perform a thorough inspection for errors. Two versions of this utility are available—a graphical version that performs basic disk-checking functions, and a command-line version that provides a much more extensive set of customization options.

> **NOTE:** *Sometimes, Check Disk will run automatically after an abnormal shutdown. It is because a specific bit in the registry is set, which indicates that the file system is "dirty". This denotes to the operating systems that that possible data was not properly written to the disk when the system was shut down. NTFS volumes keep a journal of all disk activities and use this information to recover the file system in the event of an abnormal shutdown.*

With the chkntfs command there are several syntaxes as shown in figure 7.9.

```
C:\Windows\system32\cmd.exe                                        _  □  ✕
Microsoft Windows [Version 6.1.7600]
Copyright (c) 2009 Microsoft Corporation.  All rights reserved.

C:\Users\Sean>chkntfs /?
Displays or modifies the checking of disk at boot time.

CHKNTFS volume [...]
CHKNTFS /D
CHKNTFS /T[:time]
CHKNTFS /X volume [...]
CHKNTFS /C volume [...]

  volume        Specifies the drive letter (followed by a colon),
                mount point, or volume name.
  /D            Restores the machine to the default behavior; all drives are
                checked at boot time and chkdsk is run on those that are
                dirty.
  /T:time       Changes the AUTOCHK initiation countdown time to the
                specified amount of time in seconds.  If time is not
                specified, displays the current setting.
  /X            Excludes a drive from the default boot-time check.  Excluded
                drives are not accumulated between command invocations.
  /C            Schedules a drive to be checked at boot time; chkdsk will run
                if the drive is dirty.

If no switches are specified, CHKNTFS will display if the specified drive is
dirty or scheduled to be checked on next reboot.

C:\Users\Sean>
```

Figure 7.9

You can use any combination of the following switches at the end of the command line to modify the operation of chkntfs as shown below:

/F	This option attempts to fix any errors Chkdsk detects. The disk must be locked and may require a reboot to perform a dismount of the volume you want to check.
/V	This option work differently on different volume types. On FAT32 volumes, using this option displays the name of every file in every directory during the disk check. On NTFS volumes, this option displays only cleanup messages.
/R	This option identifies bad sectors and attempt to recover data from those sectors if possible. The disk must be locked.
/I	This option performs a simpler check of index entries reducing the amount of time required to complete the check only on NTFS volumes.

/C   This option skips the checking of cycles within the folder structure and reduces the amount of time required only on NTFS volumes.

/X   This option forces the volume to dismount only on NTFS volumes.

/L[:size]   This option adjusts the size of the NTFS transactions log only on NTFS volumes.

/B   This option reevaluates bad clusters only on NTFS volumes.

/P   This option performs an exhaustive check of the disk in the Windows Recovery Environment only on NTFS volumes.

/R   This option repairs bad spots found on the disk in the Windows Recovery Environment only on NTFS volumes.

Disk Cleanup

The Disk Cleanup utility is a very quick utility to clean up the temporary files and other items that can be cleaned safely to make space. You can start this by pressing the Start Bar (Round Windows logo), then All Programs, Accessories, System Tools, then Disk Cleanup, and the Disk Cleanup: Drive Selection will come up as shown in figure 7.10.

Note: If you click any "low disk space" warning, the Disk Cleanup tool opens automatically.

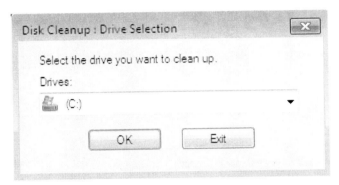

Figure 7.10

Once you choose the drive letter it will scan your drive and calculate how much space the tool can free up in the different categories. As shown in figure 7.11.

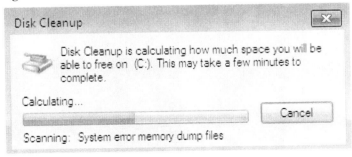

Figure 7.11

Obviously, I have a computer that is new as the total amount of free space I can free up is 19.5MB as shown in figure 7.12. But typically if the utility has not been run in some time you can free up quite a bit of space.

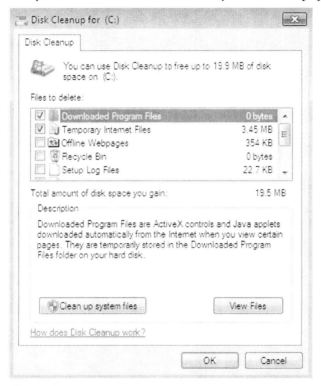

Figure 7.12

In figure 7.13 I have scrolled down to show the additional options that I can choose from on the "Files to delete" box.

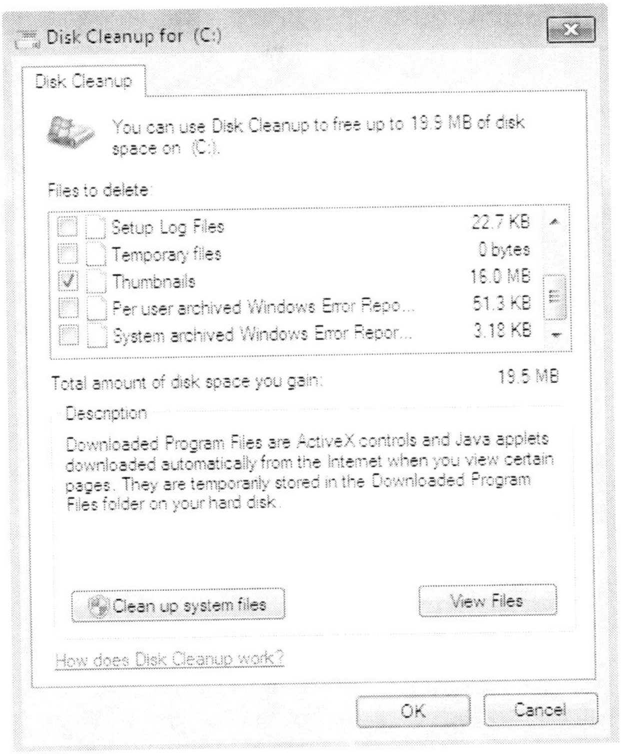

File 7.13

After all that I decided I needed to gain some space so I chose the first two options and I chose to delete the Thumbnails to give myself an extra 19.5MB of space. Once I selected those items and clicked OK, a confirmation box appeared as shown in figure 7.14.

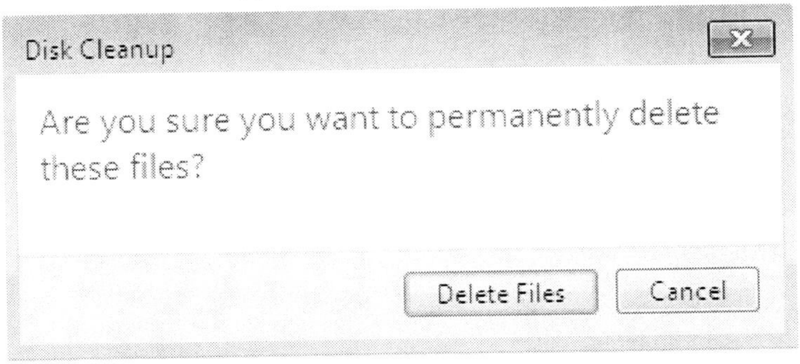

Figure 7.14

If you did an upgrade to Windows 7 or an installation of Windows it placed your old operating systems files in a folder called Windows.old. You can reclaim a lot of disk space by deleting this folder or a majority of its contents.

Advanced Boot Options

Like in previous versions of Windows there you can type in MSCONFIG at the "Search for Programs and Files" on the Start Bar and you get the System Configuration tool which you can use to identify problems that might prevent Windows from starting correctly.

This tool allows you to start Windows with common services and startup programs turned off or on. You can also experiment or troubleshoot by turning services on one at a time to help identify which services or boot line is causing a problem and help up you isolate problems.

In figure 7.15 we see the System Configuration tool and all of its tabs.

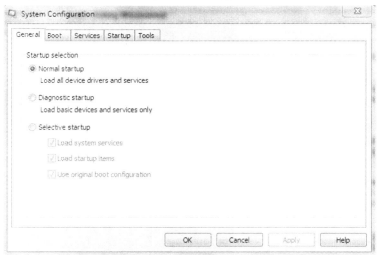

Figure 7.15

Let's take a look at each of the tabs pictured in figure 7.15 one at a time.

General Tab

The General tab lists choices for startup configuration modes which are as follows:

> **Normal startup**-This option starts Windows as it should always start in its ready state and properly working.
>
> **Diagnostic startup**-This option starts Windows with the very basic services and drivers only.
>
> **Selective startup**-This option starts Windows with basic services and drivers along with other services or startup programs that you select.

Boot Tab

This is a very important tab as seen in figure 7.16, and shows configuration options for the operating system, advanced debugging settings, allows you to use more than one processor at boot, and limit the amount of ram that can be used.

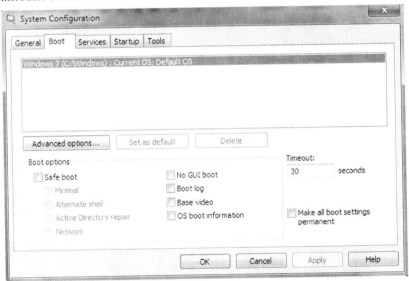

Figure 7.16

Let's look at these setting which including:

Safe boot(Minimal)-This startup option opens the Windows graphical user interface in safe mode loading only critical system drivers and services. Networking is disabled.

Safe boot(Alternate shell)- This startup option opens the Windows command prompt in safe mode. Again only running only critical system drivers and services. Networking and the graphical user interface are disabled.

Safe boot(Active Directory repair)-This startup option opens the Windows graphical user interface in safe mode loading only critical system drivers, services, and Active Directory.

Safe boot(Network)-This startup option opens the Windows graphical user interface in safe mode running only critical system drivers and services. Networking is enabled however.

No GUI boot-This startup option does not display the Windows Welcome screen at startup.

Boot log-This startup option stores all information from the startup process in the file %SystemRoot%Ntbtlog.txt on the hard drive.

Base video-This startup option opens the Windows graphical user interface in minimal VGA mode, using only standard VGA drivers.

OS boot information-This startup option Shows driver names as drivers are being loaded during the startup process.

Make all boot settings permanent-This startup option does not allow for tracking changes made in System Configuration. Options that are chosen can be changed manually in the System Configuration. If you choose this option you can't roll back your changes by selecting Normal startup on the General tab in the previous section.

Options in the Advanced Options

By pressing the Advanced Options on the Boot Tab menu, you have access to some very powerful tools such as the following:

Figure 7.17

Number of processors-This option selects the number of processors to use on boot up on multiprocessor systems as shown in figure 7.17.

Maximum memory-This option specifies the maximum amount of physical memory used by the operating system. This is helpful when you want to simulate a low memory configuration. The value in the text box is megabytes (MB).

PCI Lock-This option stops Windows from reallocating I/O and IRQ resources on the PCI bus. The I/O and memory resources set by the BIOS are preserved.

Debug-This option enables kernel-mode debugging for device driver development.

Global Debug Settings

Global debug settings are to troubleshoot a connection between the hosts a target computers using Serial, IEEE 1394, or USB 2.0 connectors. There are several option which are available:

Debug port-This option specifies you are using debugging usage of the serial port. The default port is COM 1.

Baud rate-This is an optional setting which specifies the baud rate to use when debugging the serial port. Possible baud rates are

9600, 19,200, 38,400, 57,600, or 115,200 bits per second (BPS). The default baud rate is 115,200 BPS.

Channel-This option specifies using 1394 as the debug connection type and specifies the channel number to use. The value for channel must be a decimal integer between 0 and 62, inclusive, and must match the channel number used by the host computer.

USB target name-This option specifies a string value to use when the debug type is USB. This string can be any value.

Services Tab

This tab shows a list of the services that start when the computer starts as shown in figure 7.23. It also displays the current status of each service and states whether the service is "Running" or "Stopped".

You can also enable or disable individual services at startup which helps to troubleshoot services which might be causing startup problems.

Bu selecting "Hide all Microsoft services" you can see only third-party services installed on the computer. You can also clear the check box for a service to disable it the next time you start the computer.

Chapter 8 - Windows Backup

Many people don't see the value of using the backup utility until their hard disk crashes or the passenger side window in their car is on the ground and their laptop bag is missing. Almost everyone has work, personal pictures, or even music that they would miss if their computer or laptop was gone. People seem to understand backing up servers but backing up their PC's just does not occur to them. It almost takes a catastrophic loss of their data to start backing it up. By then it is too late.

In this section we will look at the following:

- How to configure a backup

- How create a disk image

- How to back up the Registry

- How to create a recovery disc

Configuring a backup

When you save things to your laptop, install software on your PC or make changes to your computer, it brings a certain level of risk. Timely, complete, and functional backups allow you to minimize that risk. The Backup and Restore utility in Windows 7 allows you to backup and restore either your selected files all the files on the operating system.

There are several ways to Backup and Restore Center. One of the easiest is to press the Start button and type backup, then select Backup and Restore as shown in figure 8.1.

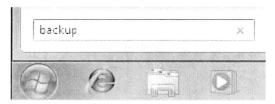

Figure 8.1

You can also open up the Control Panel and select System and Security and select Backup and Restore as shown in figure 8.2.

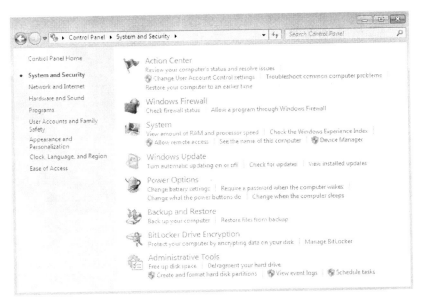

Figure 8.2

After you click on the Backup and Restore button you will see the Backup utility screen shown in figure 8.3.

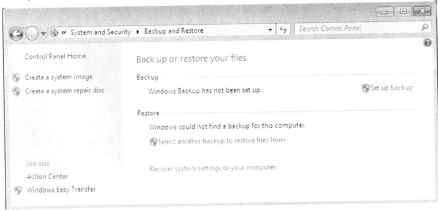

Figure 8.3

To backup your files, first click the "Set up backup..." button.

Windows will now prepare your system for backup and present you with a list of all the media it has found to perform a backup as shown below in figure 8.4. You will notice that I have selected the FreeAgent USB drive using drive E:.

> **NOTE:** *To restore a file form a backup, launch Backup and Restore and click Restore Files. Locate the backup media your files are stored on and follow the instructions to get your previously backed up files back.*

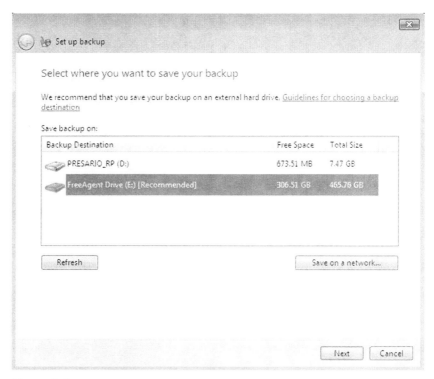

Figure 8.4

NOTE: *If you have a CD ROM/DVD Writer installed you will have the option to write the backup to that location as well. There is no additional software needed.*

I tend to know what I want to back up so I choose, "Let me choose" as shown in figure 8.5. But if you are unsure or have very little administration experience with backing up data with one or previous versions of Windows, I would select the first option which allows Windows to decide what should be backed up.

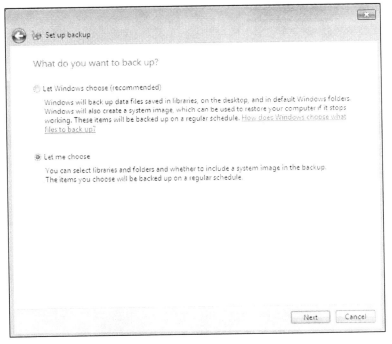

Figure 8.5

The next screen that appears in figure 8.6 allows you to choose what you would like to backup by placing a checkmark next to the item I want to backup.

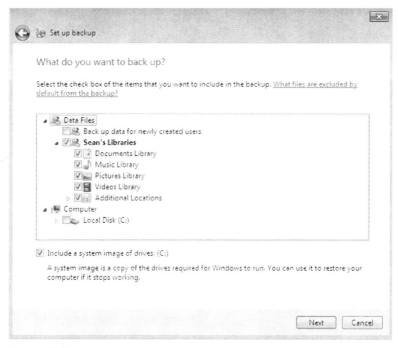

Figure 8.6

After you click Next, there is just one last screen that appears to allow us to review all the settings we have selected as shown in Figure 8.7.

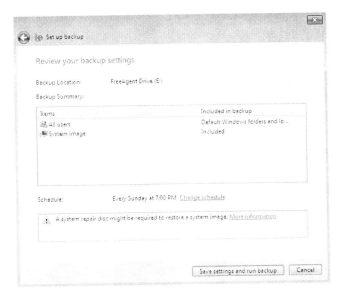

Figure 8.7

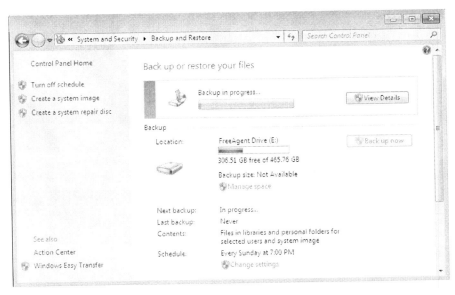

Figure 8.8

In figure 8.8, you see that our backup is about five percent complete. This is a running progress bar. Also below the backup in progress status bar you see the drive you are backing your data up to and the amount of free space still available. It is a blue bar unless the space available on the drive becomes less than ten percent and then it will turn red.

When the backup is running you will see a small clock on the flag in to the Superbar as shown below in figure 8.9.

Figure 8.9

When your backup is completed you can go back and edit the settings to configure the frequency of your backup and make it an automated process. You can set how often, the day, and the time as shown below in figure 8.10. I do recommend however that if you rely on this process to work, check to make sure the backup has run on a regular basis. I would also do a test restore which to make sure that what you are backing up is restorable.

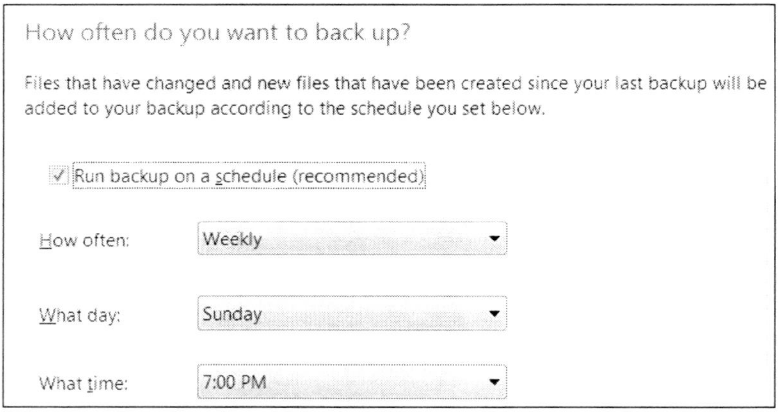

How often do you want to back up?

Files that have changed and new files that have been created since your last backup will be added to your backup according to the schedule you set below.

☑ Run backup on a schedule (recommended)

How often: Weekly ▼

What day: Sunday ▼

What time: 7:00 PM ▼

Figure 8.10

Create System Image

A system image is one of the fastest ways to restore your hard disk. This is different than a backup which you select the data you want to backup. If you do a restore it is done on an operating system that is functioning well enough to do the restore. A system images an exact copy of the disk or partition at the time the image was made.

It is also an excellent way of installing the same configuration and software on multiple PC's. You can install the operating system and all the software on one PC or laptop, create an image and then you can copy that image to all the other new PC's or laptops. From a DVD it takes about 10-20 minutes to install the PC's.

> **NOTE:** *You should not activate Windows on the PC or laptop you are creating the image from. That way you can activate the Windows key that came with each individual PC or laptop.*

To create an image, first on the Backup and Restore menu in the Control Panel you will see the "Create a system image" link on the left as shown in figure 8.11.

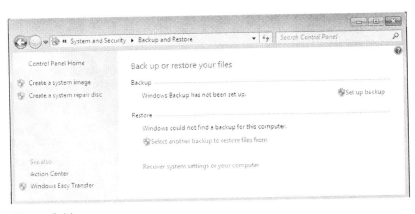

Figure 8.11

Once you click on the link in figure 8.10, you will get a screen that allows you to choose where you would like the image to be stored. You will see that I have a 300GB FreeAgent USB drive attached which I have chosen to place the system image on this drive. But along with attached drives, you have the option to place it on DVD or to a network location as well as shown in figure 8.12.

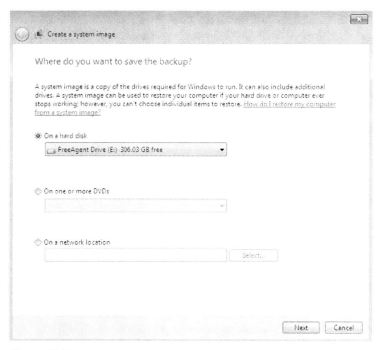

Figure 8.12

After you have selected a media location that has enough space for the image, Windows 7 will give you a confirmation screen before starting as shown in figure 8.13. It will also display the drive letters of the drives you will be creating an image of.

Figure 8.13

The image will start by clicking the Start Backup button as shown in figure 8.14.

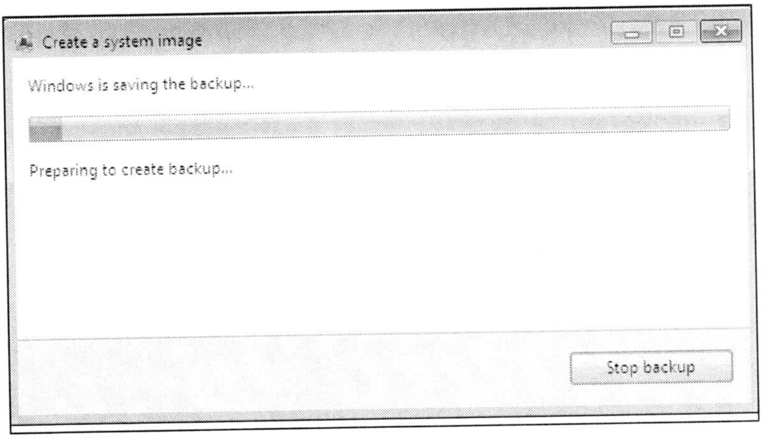

Figure 8.14

Backing up the Registry

Occasionally, when troubleshooting or making changes to the operating system, you will have to make changes to the registry and it might become corrupt. Some troubleshooting steps require you to change values in your registry. If you make a mistake and don't correct it, you may find your computer no longer functions as it did before. To protect yourself from any mistakes or other system problems, you need to backup your registry.

To backup the registry, first open the registry by going to the Start button and then type regedit as shown in Figure 8.15.

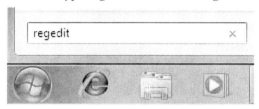

Figure 8.15

Then left click Computer in the left side pane as shown in figure 8.16.

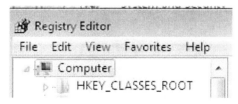

Figure 8.16

Next, choose File and then Export. A window similar to the one in figure 8.17 will appear. Choose the location you want to save the file and then press Save.

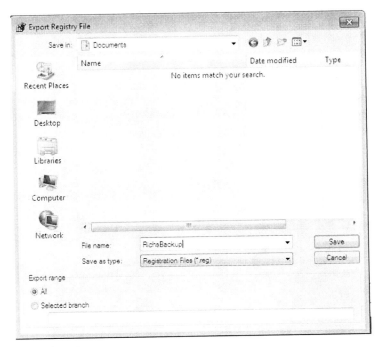

Figure 8.17

NOTE: *To restore the registry follow the same instructions but choose Import instead of Export.*

Create a System Recovery Disc

If Windows 7 becomes corrupt you can avoid a full installation of the operating system by having a System Recovery Disc. You can use this disc to attempt a repair at boot up. The system recovery disc cannot be used to install or reinstall Windows, but it can be used to fix common problems that prevent Windows from booting.

To create a system recovery disc, do the following. First, open the Backup and Restore utility and then click the link called, "Create a system repair disc". As shown in figure 8.18.

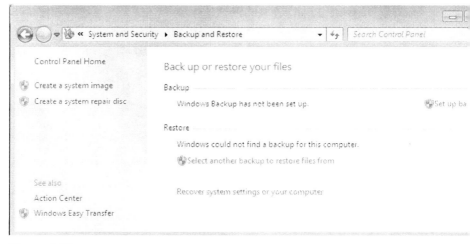

Figure 8.18

After you click on the link, the screen shown in figure 8.19 will appear and allow you to select your DVD drive. Once you have selected the drive, click Create disc.

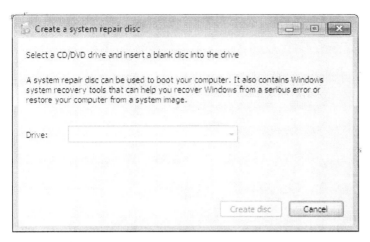

Figure 8.19

NOTE: *You will need a blank writable DVD to make the disc.*

Chapter 9 – Other New Windows 7 Features

Windows 7 is packed with a whole host of new features. In this chapter, we'll take a look at some of these new features which we have not covered already in this book. We will look at how they can help you work more efficiently on your computer. This is not an exhaustive break down of each feature; but it will bring an awareness of what Windows 7 has to offer.

In this chapter we will cover:

- Federated Search
- Snip Tool
- Sticky Notes
- Personal Character Edition
- Device Stage
- ReadyBoost
- Branch Cache
- Internet Explorer

Federated Search

The new Federated Search tool is used to search beyond the scope of your local PC hard drives for relevant content. It is based on OpenSearch and RSS to allow you to search remote repositories. You can use third party search connectors or create your own connectors, which is very easy because of the standard format used by OpenSearch. An example is created in Appendix C of this book.

There are already many search connectors available for you to download from:

- Bing (I created in Appendix C)

- Deviant Art Search

- Flickr Search Connector

- Google Blogs Search Connector

- Google News Search Connector

- Microsoft Windows Live Search Connector

- MSN Search

- Twitter Search Connector

- YouTube Search Connector

As more sites add support for OpenSearch, expect to see more search connectors emerging for Windows 7. I am sure with the ease of creating a search connector the list of available Federated Search tools will be as long as this book is.

Sidebar: What is Open Search?

OpenSearch is a collection of simple formats for the sharing of search results. You can use OpenSearch formats to help people discover relevant content search results across the web. It's like having your own personal search engine, but others can create search tools to search their own personal or corporate libraries.

The Internet is a big place, and search engines only crawl the surface of the web and only find a small fraction of the great content that is out there. Moreover, some of the richest and most interesting content cannot even be crawled and indexed by one search engine.

OpenSearch also helps search engines and search clients communicate by introducing a common set of formats to perform search requests and syndicate search results.

You might be surprised that OpenSearch was created by A9.com, which ix an Amazon.com company, and the OpenSearch format is now in use by hundreds of search engines and search applications on the Internet.

I went ahead and created a Search Connector for Microsoft's Bing.com search engine. In Appendix C of this book, you can see the steps I used, links to learn how to do it yourself and you can copy my code until your heart is content. It took me about three hours to create the code for which I saved as Bing.osdx on the desktop as shown in figure 9.1.

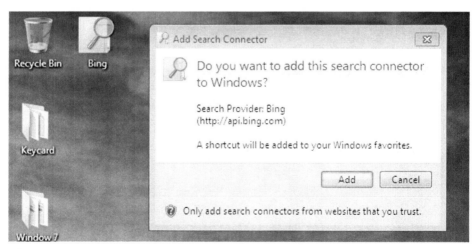

Figure 9.1

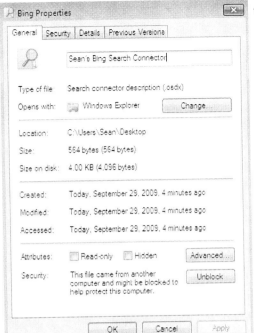

If I right click on the file you will see the properties in figure 9.2.

Figure 9.2

You see in figure 9.1, I have also clicked on the icon for the Bing search connector I created and it asks me if it is Ok to install. I clicked the Add button and it installs in only a few seconds. I now have a new search connector under favorites in my Libraries as shown below in figure 9.3.

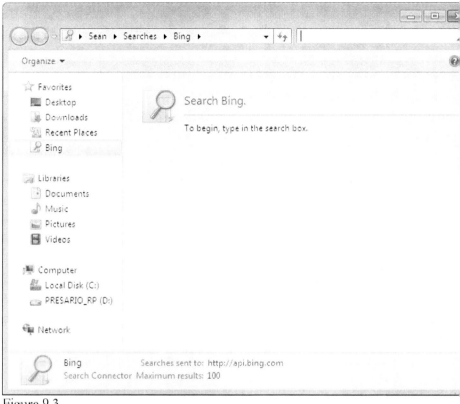

Figure 9.3

Snip Tool

One of the coolest little additions to Windows Vista and carried over to Windows 7 is the Snipping Tool. This tool allows you to move your mouse and take a picture of as large of a square of your screen as you would like and make it in to a picture. It then can be saved as a picture or copied to a document. Down below you will see that I have several Sticky Notes on my desktop. If I did a Shift+Print Screen, I would get the entire screen. But the Snipping Tool allows me to highlight only the area I want to copy as shown in figure 9.4. Here I have only copied the Sticky notes and not the entire desktop screen. I can also write or draw a picture on the already captured picture or erase parts that I don't want as well. A very fun little tool.

Figure 9.4

Sticky Notes

This is another fun little tool included with Windows 7. We are all familiar with the Post It notes we have on our desks. Well Windows 7 makes them go digital. Put little reminders on your screen and even use it as your task list. If you want another Post It, click the "+" sign. They will continue across your screen as shown in figure 9.5. If they run out of room they will overlap. If you are done with one, click the "X" and delete it. The cool thing is that if you shut off your computer, they will be back just like you left them on your desktop. The ones in figure 9.6 have been on my desktop for weeks.

Figure 9.5

Figure 9.6

192

Personal Character Editor

Have you ever wanted to create your own font characters? Well here is
your chance with the Personal Character Edition included in Windows 7
under Accessories. You can use this feature to create your own letters
and font. Simply click on the boxes where you want to illuminate pixels
as shown in figure 9.7.

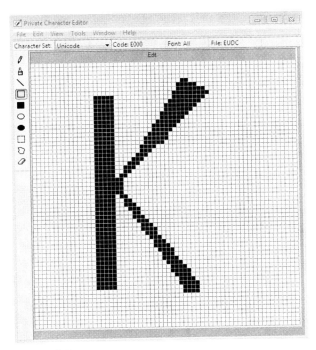

Figure 9.7

Jump Lists

Jump Lists are a new feature in Windows 7. Jump Lists don't just show shortcuts to files, they are items that you go to frequently. Once you have opened a document, music, or any other file, if you right click on the icon on the Superbar it will show the items you recently opened. If you hover over an item with your mouse and a pushpin will appear on the right of the line you're hovering over. Click the pushpin on the right and you will pin that on the Jump List. This means that item will always be there when you restart Windows or log off and then back on. (You can click again to unpin as well.)

Let's take a look at an example. In figure 9.8 you see the documents I have recently opened. I am working on the Windows 7 Administrators Black Book and I have been frequently opening it.

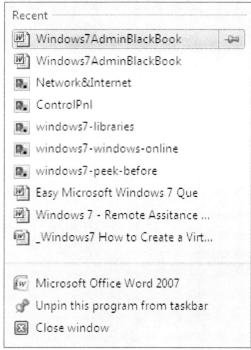

Figure 9.8

Since I have just started on the book I need to open it a lot and I don't want to search the hard drive for my document and waste time. So I am

194

going to click on the pushpin to the right as shown in figure 9.9. From here on regardless of how many times I log off and log on or open other documents, the items I push a pushpin on will always be there.

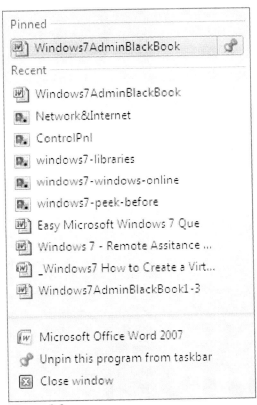

Figure 9.9

You can also pin applications to the Start Bar and also pin documents to those application as shown below in figure 9.10.

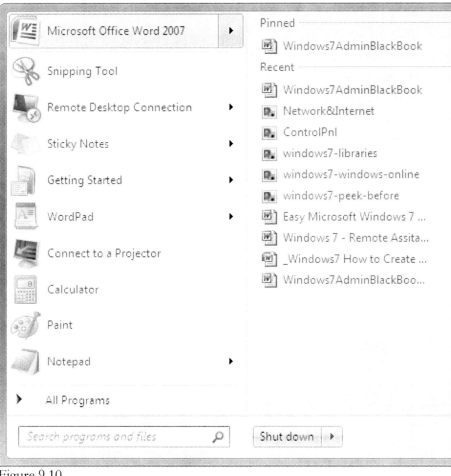

Figure 9.10

ReadyBoost

Remember when your old computer got slow because there was not enough RAM? You had to go run to the computer store and find these little RAM sticks that gave you more RAM and made your PC faster. Not anymore! Now you can use a thumb drive? What? No kidding. I increased the Physical Memory of the Windows 7 PC I am using by 2GB by using a blank solid state thumb drive and ReadyBoost.

If you plug a ReadyBoost-compatible storage device into your computer, the AutoPlay dialog box offers you the option to install ReadyBoost.

Once you select the option to install ReadyBoost, Windows shows you how much space you should use on the drive with a recommendation for optimal performance as shown in figure 9.11.

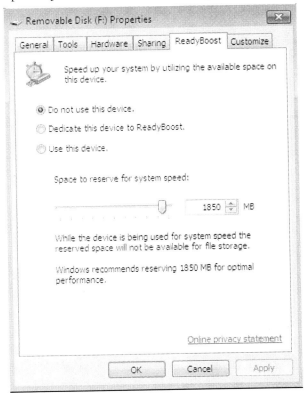

Figure 9.11

Next, choose the second or third options to use the device for ReadyBoost. If you will be using the device for ReadyBoost only, you can choose the second option as shown in figure 9.12 and use all the available

space on the drive. If you choose the last option you can use the scroll
bar to choose how much space to dedicate to physical memory.

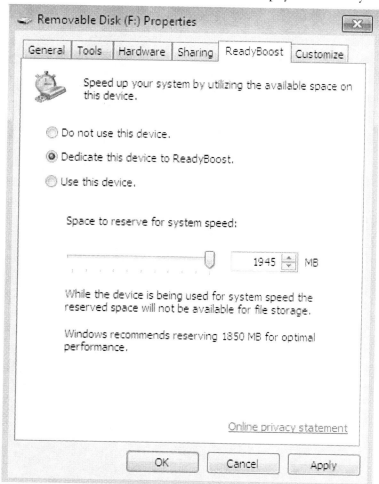

Figure 9.12

It's really easy to use Windows ReadyBoost. And if the ReadyBoost device
is not present it will not harm the operation of the Windows operating
system. You can use almost any removable memory device such as a USB
flash drive or a secure digital (SD) memory card.

ReadyBoost was originally introduced in Windows Vista but was a little
known feature. There was a 4GB restriction in Windows Vista but that
has been removed so larger flash drives can be used. The limit of one

ReadyBoost device has also been removed which gives users the possibility to use multiple flash drives as additional caches in Windows 7. In figure 9.12 you see the new ReadyBoost drive shown as Disk1 on the Computer Managements, Disk Management option.

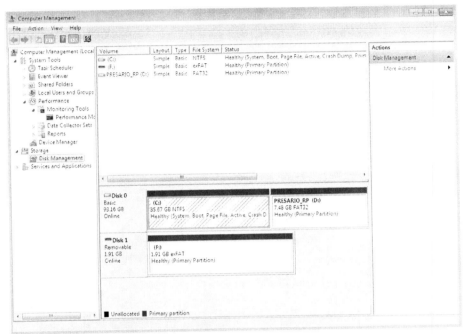

Figure 9.12

Branch Cache

Windows BranchCache is included in Windows Server 2008 R2 and Windows 7. BranchCache is a new feature and is not based on the ISA server as many people believe.

Basically this feature allows a client to only read content from a peer (or hosted cache server) which matches the content hashes the client retrieved from the original content server.

Meaning that the host server will download content once for the original requesting client and then cache a copy of the same material.

> **Alert**: *It appears that the BranchCache service takes over port 80 which interferes with using Apache on a workstation.*

Configure Branch Cache Server

BranchCache, focused mainly on optimizing your WAN bandwidth using special cache options available only in Windows Server 2008 R2. BranchCache works in scenarios with branch offices where clients interact and request files from a central location such as a headquarters.

BranchCache is a simple idea that caches the content downloaded from the central location using a server or other branch clients. Every time that a second client tries to download the content, the request is directly handled within the branch office optimizing the WAN link and downloading time.

There are no complex configurations and you can even use an option that does not include a server. There are two types of BranchCache deployment options: Distributed Cache (no server) and Hosted Cache Mode (Windows Server 2008 R2 server).

> **Alert:** *Distributed Cache environment will only work with Windows Server 2008 R2 and Windows 7 clients.*

To configure the Windows 2008 R2 file server to be a BranchCache server, select the Add Features Wizard in the Server Manager and select BranchCache as shown in figure 9.13.

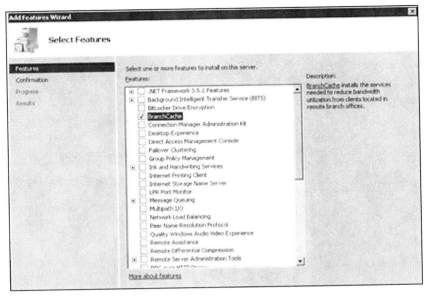

Figure 9.13

File Services role and the service must be selected to handle BranchCache for remote files as shown in figure 9.14.

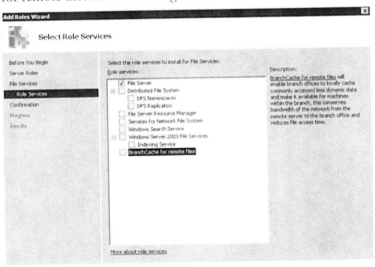

Figure 9.14

You must now configure Group Policy (GPO) to enable BranchCache.

> **NOTE:** *Active Directory is recommended but not a requirement for BranchCache.*

You can use an Active Directory or local policy to apply to this server. The GPO can be located in the Computer Configuration, Policies, Administrative Templates, Network, Lanman Server, and Hash Publication for BranchCache as shown in figure 9.15.

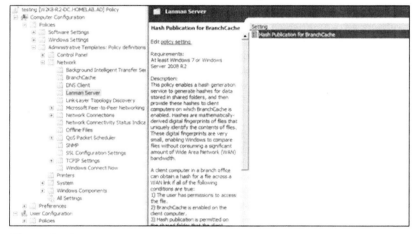

Figure 9.15

When you click on the, "Hash Publication for BranchCache" option you will get the screen in figure 9.16 which allows you to enable BranchCache. Click on Enable and select, "Allow hash publication for all file servers."

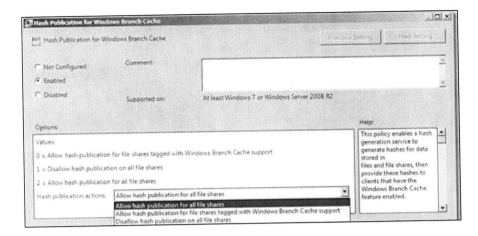

Figure 9.16

BranchCache Client Configuration

On the Windows 7 Client it is pretty easy to configure as well. First you need to configure the GPO by editing the settings in the MMC. You do this by going to Computer Configuration, Policies, Administrative Templates, Network, Turn on BranchCache, and then enable the option as shown in figure 9.17.

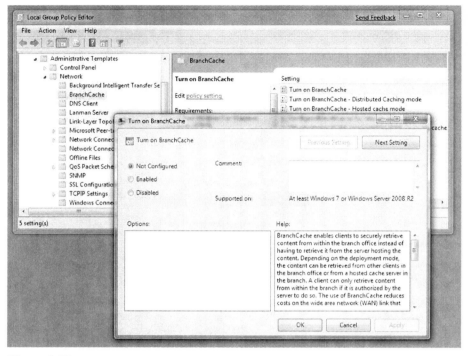

Figure 9.17

Also in figure 9.17 you need to set several other options. If you are using Distributed Cache, enable "Turn on BranchCache – Distributed Caching Mode". Or if you are using hosted cache mode you will need to enable, "Turn on BranchCache" and select "Hosted Cache mode".

Optionally, you can also set other values using this set of GPOs, like latency values or setting a percentage of your disk space dedicated to this cache. Also you will need to ensure that you have configured the firewall inbound policies to allow BranchCache connections. 3. Configure the Cache Server

For more information you can go to:

http://www.microsoft.com/downloads/details.aspx?displaylang=en&FamilyID=a9a1ed8a-71ab-468e-a7e0-470fd46e46b3

Internet Explorer 8

Internet Explorer 8 is Microsoft's latest web browser, which comes packed with many new features. Below is an explanation of how to get IE8 up and running and use some of the new features.

Let's take a look at a few new features including Quick Tabs and In Private viewing features.

Quick Tabs

The Quick Tabs button is the 4 little boxes with the down arrow next to the left of the tabs. They show you all currently open tabs at a glance to help you select the page you need. Each tab shows a scaled down window of the current website you are viewing as shown in figure 9.18.

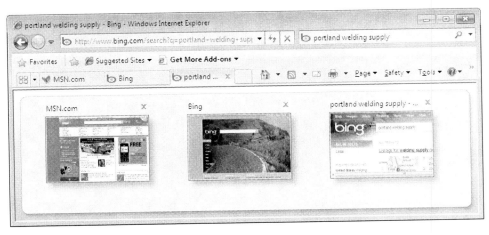

Figure 9.18

Improved Search

The search feature has been greatly improved, with smart suggestions and even an inline search as shown in figure 9.19.

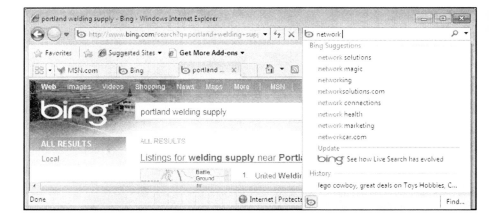

InPrivate Browsing

InPrivate Browsing helps prevent websites from and Internet Explorer from obtaining or storing data about your browsing sessions. This includes cookies, temporary Internet files, history, and Windows 7 Features other data. Toolbars and extensions are disabled by default when you use this feature.

To turn on this feature go to Safety and select InPrivate browsing as shown in figure 9.20.

Note: *To turn off the feature repeat the same process.*

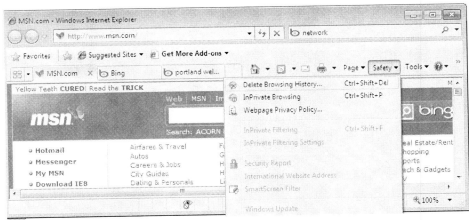

Figure 9.20

In figure 9.21, you will notice the new InPrivate logo next to the address in the Address Toolbar on the browser.

Figure 9.21

Chapter 10 – Devices and Printers

Windows 7 makes installing devices and printers about as easy as you can make it. Unlike with Windows XP when Windows Vista came out we had to wait for a lot of plug and play device and printer drivers. In Windows 7, all Vista 32 and 64 bit drivers are compatible. Notice in figure 10.1, I have no printers installed except for the default Microsoft XPS Document writer. But in real like I have an HP OfficeJet 1300n and a Lexmark 7350. In this section we will walk through installing my HP OfficeJet 1300n. We will also look at changing the printer properties as well.

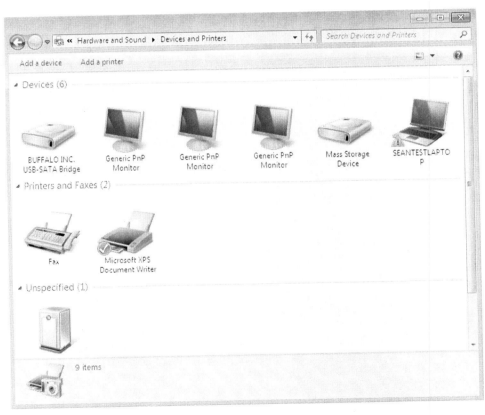

Figure 10.1

Installing a Printer or Device

First, I am going to go to Start, Control Panel, Hardware and Sound as shown in figure 10.2 below.

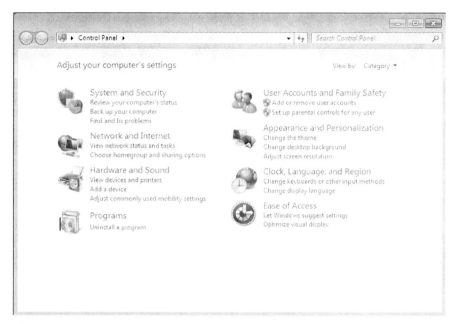

Figure 10.2

Next, unlike going to Printers like previous Windows versions I am going to choose add a device and I see the screen shown in figure 10.3.

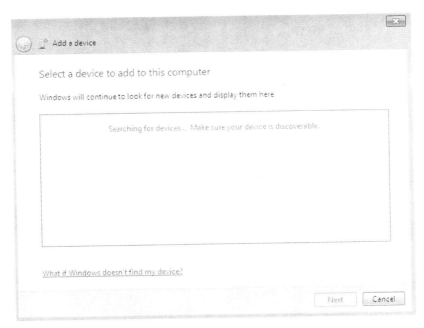

Figure 10.3

Next, I am simply going to plug in the printer and Windows should give you an acknowledgement as show in figure 10.4. I am using printers that had drivers built in to Widows 7. If I bought a new printer or a device that did not have a driver that was built in, you would either need to download the Vista or Windows 7 driver from the Internet or install them from a CD or DVD. It is always safer to install the driver for the printer or the device before plugging the device in.

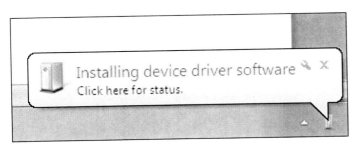

Figure 10.4

If the printer driver does not match a plug and play device you will see the window shown in figure 10.5 to allow you to either select the printer or select, "Have Disk..." to install the driver if you have one.

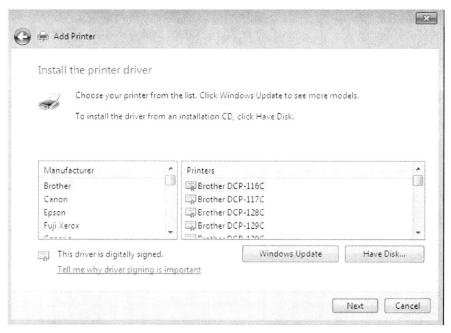

Figure 10.5

The printer I am installing already has a plug and play driver so I get a pop up asking me which driver to install as shown in figure 10.6.

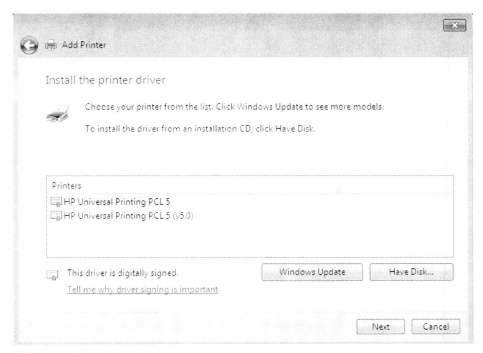

Figure 10.6

Next, I receive a screen to identify a name that I will use to identify this printer as shown in figure 10.7.

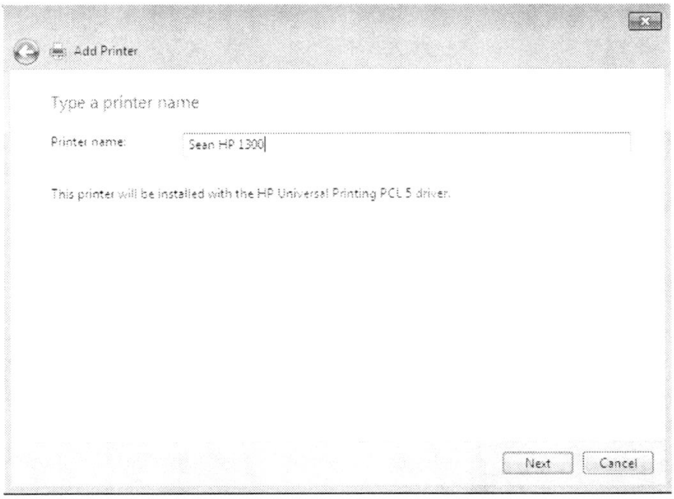

Figure 10.7

When you enter a name and click Next. You will then see the following screen indicating the printer is installing in figure 10.8.

Figure 10.8

The next screen you will see will indicate that you have installed the printer successfully and give you the option to print a test page as shown in figure 10.9.

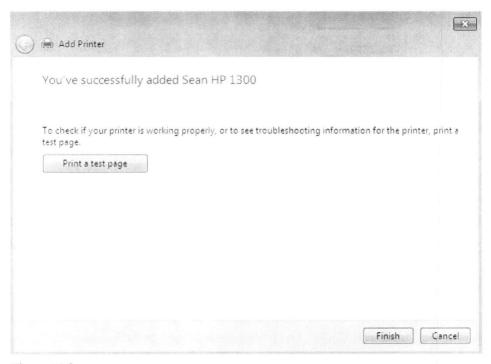

Figure 10.9

Printer Properties

Windows 7 allows device manufacturers to create their own properties pages as you can see from the Properties page shown below in figure 10.10. This is a screenshot from my Lexmark 7350 printer.

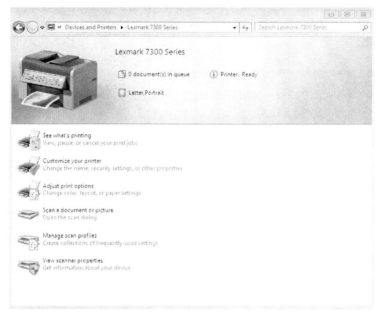

Figure 10.10

The screens that manufacturers can create are very graphical as shown on figure 10.11.

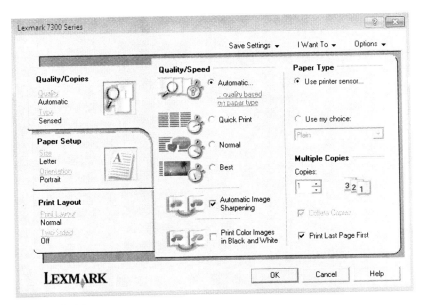

Figure 10.11

Now that we have seen the Properties for the Lexmark printer, let's take a look at the typical properties screen as shown in figure 10.12 Printing Shortcuts tab.

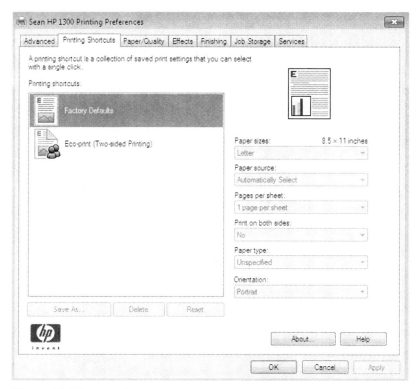

Figure 10.12

The General Tab is where you can identify the location of the printer, a description, or try a test print as shown below in figure 10.13.

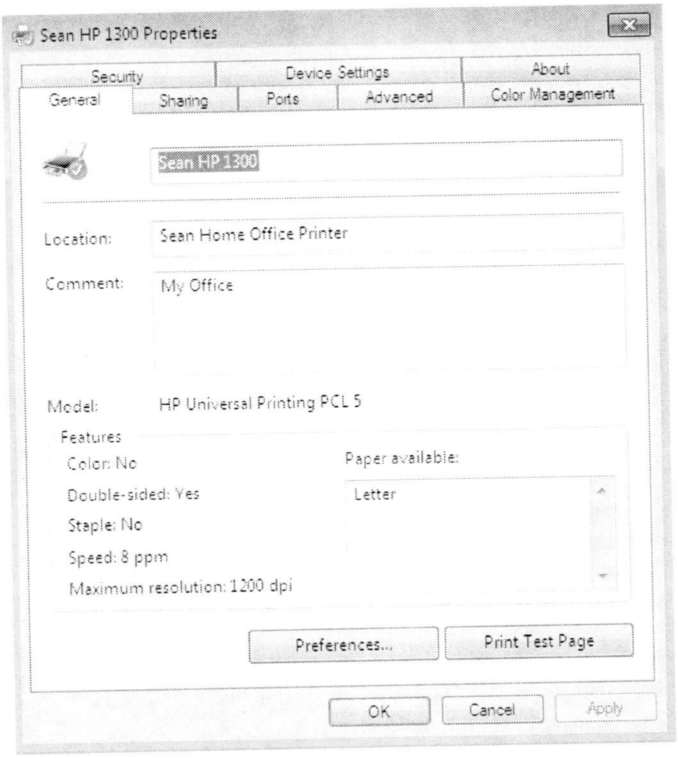

Figure 10.13

The rest of the tabs are pretty similar to those found in previous versions of Windows. For more information on each item please see:

http://windows.Microsoft.com/en-US/windows7/Choosing-print-options

219

Chapter 11 – Fun Stuff

Microsoft has really gone out of their way to make Windows 7 fun for every age group. They have created games that everyone can enjoy and made the quite good, both visually and functionally. I have seen the offices where everyone is playing Solitaire on a Friday afternoon waiting to go home. Well they have a lot more to play with now. And with a lot more features.

The trouble a user might have is the new AppLocker feature in Windows 7 which may keep users from being non-productive playing the new games. The feature allows an administrator to disallow any programs or applications that he or she does not want to allow running on their PC in the network. And it appears Windows won't install the games by default either. So users have some hurtles they have overcome.

Well if you are reading this section we are going to first explain how to install the games. Then we will look at the games that come with Windows 7 in three categories which are Internet games, board games, and children's games. Last we will look at how to get access to over 1,000 other games from Microsoft to install or use on Windows 7. Yikes. Business owners are cringing all over, I can feel it.

Installing Games on Windows 7

It's actually a pretty easy process to install the dames if you have the installation DVD. (I can see I am instructing a million employees everywhere on how to grab their Windows 7 DVD and install the games on their PC's at work.

After you have inserted the Windows 7 DVD, go to Start and then the Control Panel, and then Programs as shown in figure 11.1.

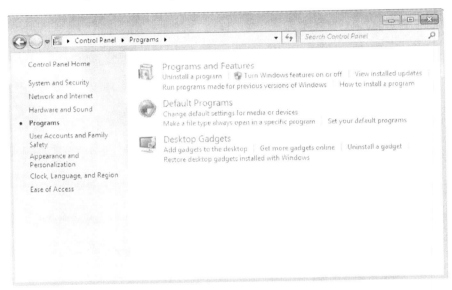

Figure 11.1

Then choose Turn Windows Features on or off as shown in figure 11.2.

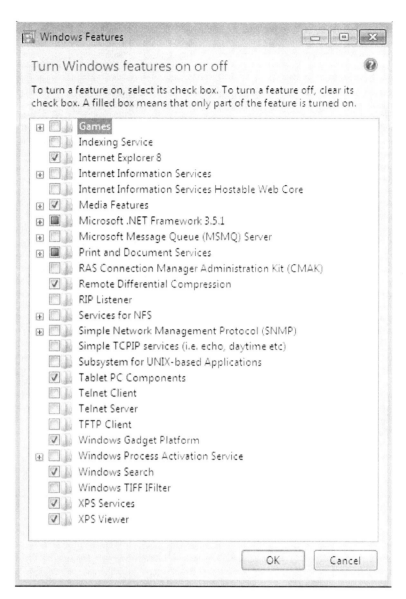

Figure 11.2

Now expand the Games and place and clock the box next to games which will automatically select all the games to install as shown in figure 11.3.

222

Figure 11.3

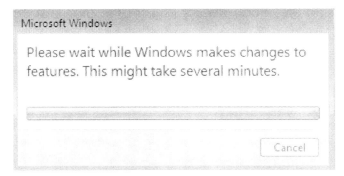

Figure 11.4

In figure 11.4 we see the results of clicking OK and continuing. On my PC it took about 2 minutes to install the new games and that was it. Not too hard to install. The games no longer show up in Accessories under Programs in the Start Menu as they did in previous versions. They have their own folder as shown in figure 11.5.

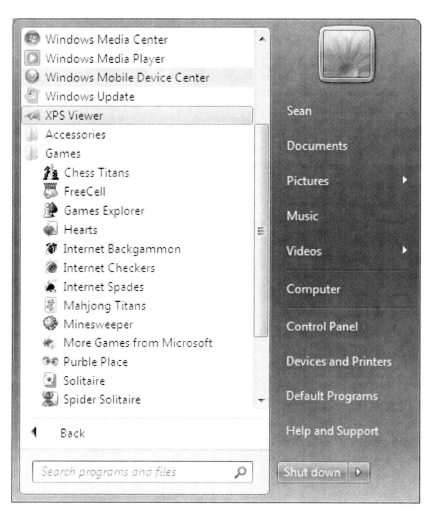

Figure 11.5

You see the games in the Start Menu under games but there is a Games Explorer as well to see the games in a graphical view as shown in figure 11.6.

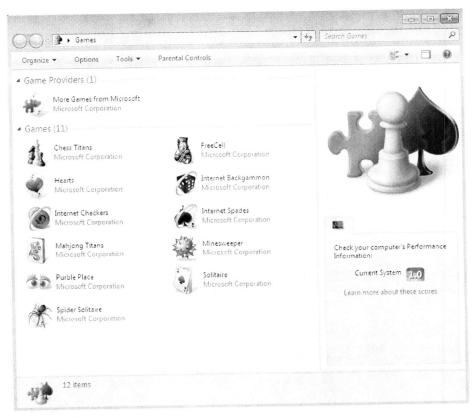

Figure 11.6

Let's take a look at these new games in the next three sections.

Internet Games

Microsoft has made it easy to play games against other opponents of the same skill level on the Internet. Each game includes a chat system with the games as well. But don't worry about your kids using it. It only allows preconfigured chat messages and you cannot identify who you are, where you're from, or any personal information whatsoever. All you can do is play a good game with someone. Let's take a look at the Internet games that come with Windows 7. Microsoft has done a good job at teaching you how to play. In fact every game opens up with an option to learn about how to play the games. The following information came from Microsoft on the numbers of players, difficulty levels and the number of players.

Internet Backgammon

Backgammon is a two-person board game with a straightforward goal: be the first to move all your pieces around and off the board as shown in figure 11.7.

- Number of players: 2
- Difficulty levels: Beginner, intermediate, expert
- Typical playing time: 10 to 30 minutes

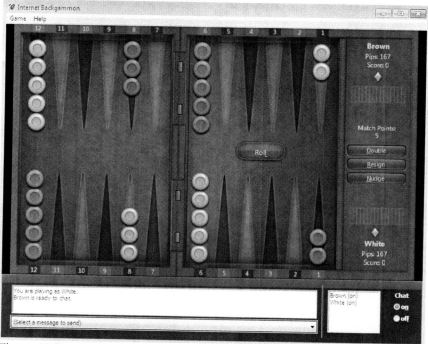

Figure 11.7

Internet Checkers

One of the oldest and most popular games in the world is back and better than ever as shown in figure 11.8.

- Number of players: 2
- Difficulty levels: Beginner, intermediate, expert
- Typical playing time: 10 to 20 minutes

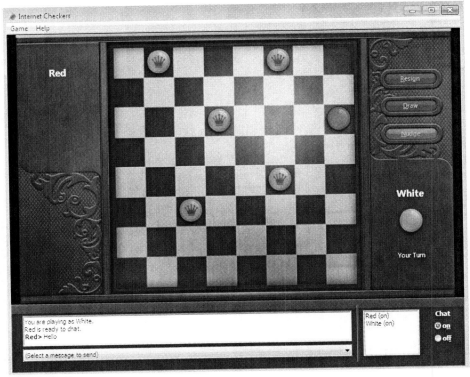

Figure 11.8

Internet Spades

Spades is a popular, fast-paced card game that demands teamwork and strategy. You guess how many "tricks" or rounds that you and your partner will win as shown in Figure 11.9.

- Number of players: 4
- Difficulty levels: Beginner, intermediate, expert
- Typical playing time: 10 to 30 minutes

Figure 11.9

Board games

There are a few board games included on the Windows 7 DVD. In this section we will take a look at each of them.

Microsoft has done a good job at teaching you how to play. In fact every game opens up with an option to learn about how to play the games. There is also a nice set of instructions in Windows Help as well. Just go to the Start menu, Support and Help and type games. The following information on the board games came from Microsoft on the description, numbers of players, difficulty levels and the number of players.

Chess Titans

Chess Titans, brings the classic strategy game of chess to life with three-dimensional graphics and animations. Highlighted squares show where your pieces can move. Choose a porcelain, marble, or wooden board, and rotate it any way you like. Chess Titans as shown in figure 10.10 is available in premium editions of Windows 7.

- Number of players: 1 or 2
- Difficulty levels: 1 (beginner) to 10 (expert)
- Typical playing time: 10 to 60 minutes

Figure 10.10

Minesweeper

Minesweeper as shown in figure 10.11 is a deceptively simple test of memory and reasoning. The goal is to uncover empty squares and avoid hidden mines.

- Number of players: 1
- Difficulty levels: Beginner, intermediate, advanced
- Typical playing time: 1 to 10 minutes

Figure 10.11

Mahjong Titans

Mahjong Titans as shown in figure 10.12, is a solitaire game played with tiles. Remove matching pairs of tiles from the board. Remove them all and you win! Mahjong Titans is available on premium editions of Windows 7.

- Number of players: 1
- Difficulty levels: Varies by tile layout
- Typical playing time: 10 to 30 minutes

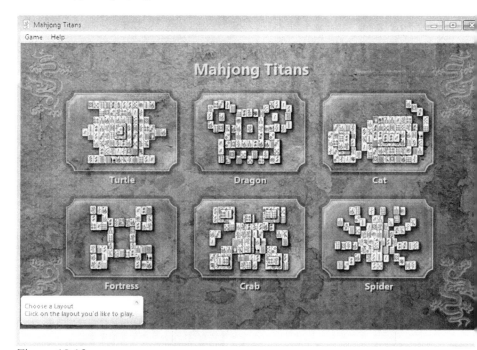

Figure 10.12

Card games

There are a number of card games included on the Windows 7 DVD. In this section we will take a look at each of them.

Microsoft has done a good job at teaching you how to play the card games. In fact every game opens up with an option to learn about how to play the games. There is also a nice set of instructions in Windows Help as well. You can see these by going to the Start menu, Support and Help and type games. The following information on the board games came from Microsoft on the description, numbers of players, difficulty levels and the number of players.

FreeCell Game

FreeCell is as shown in figure 11.13 is a form of solitaire played with a single deck.

- Number of players: 1
- Difficulty levels: One level
- Typical playing time: 10 to 20 minutes

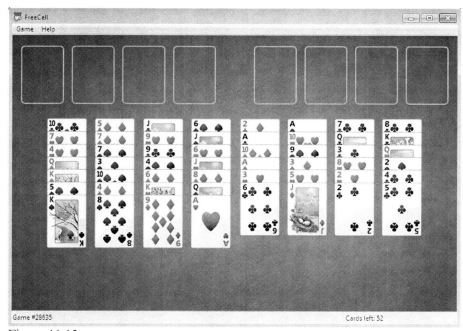

Figure 11.13

Hearts Game

Hearts as shown in figure 11.14 is a card game that you play in rounds against three computer opponents.

- Number of players: 1 (against 3 computer opponents)
- Difficulty levels: One level
- Typical playing time: 10 to 20 minutes

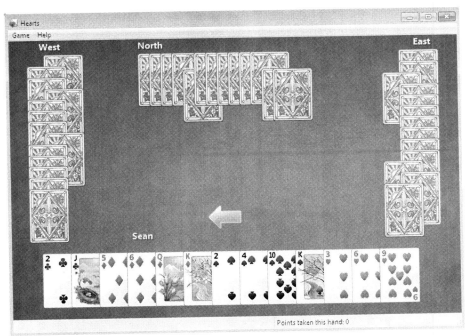

Figure 11.14

Solitaire Game

Solitaire as shown in figure 11.16 is based on the most popular variant of solitaire, Klondike. You can change the look of the cards by going to Game and Change Appearance as shown in figure 11.15.

Number of players: 1
Difficulty levels: One level
Typical playing time: 1 to 15 minutes

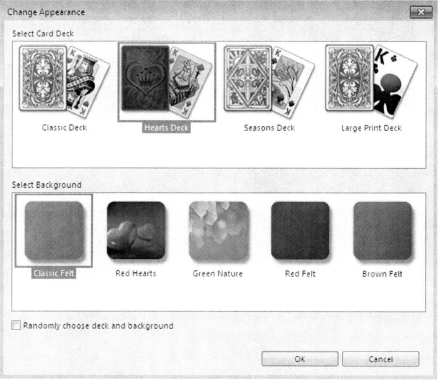

Figure 11.15

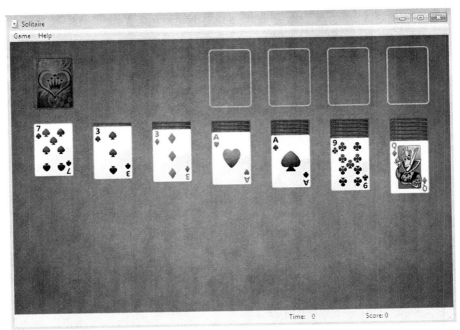

Figure 11.15

Spider Solitaire Game

Spider Solitaire as shown in figure 11.18 is a variant of solitaire that uses two decks' worth of cards instead of one. Just like in Solitaire you can change the face of the cards as shown in figure 11.17.

- Number of players: 1
- Difficulty levels: Beginner, intermediate, advanced
- Typical playing time: 1 to 15 minutes

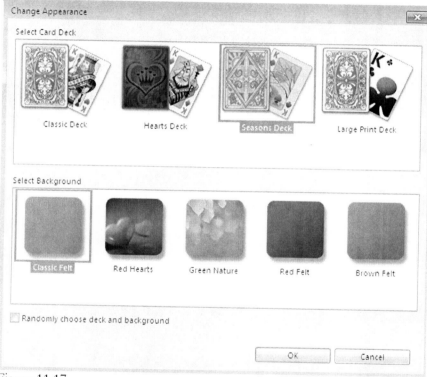

Figure 11.17

Figure 11.18

Children's Games

Purble Place is a three in one game which includes: Comfy Cakes, Purble Shop, and Purble Pairs. This game teaches children memory, pattern recognition, and reasoning skills.

Microsoft has done a good job at teaching you how to play the card games. In fact every game opens up with an option to learn about how to play the games. There is also a nice set of instructions in Windows Help as well. You can see these by going to the Start menu, Support and Help and type games. The following information on the children's games came from Microsoft on the description, numbers of players, difficulty levels and the number of players.

Below you will see the start screen for Purble Place in figure 11.19. Each building you see in the picture takes you to one of the games.

Figure 11.19

Comfy Cakes

This game shown in figure 11.20, puts you in Chef Purble's bakery, where you must complete an order for a batch of cakes. The bakery's customers are very picky and the cakes must be made exactly as ordered.

- Number of players: 1
- Difficulty levels: Beginner, intermediate, advanced
- Typical playing time: 1 to 5 minutes

Figure 11.20

Purble Shop

This game shown in figure 11.21, tests your powers of deduction. The goal is to make your Purble's face match the mystery Purble behind the curtain.

- Number of players: 1
- Difficulty levels: Beginner, intermediate, advanced
- Typical playing time: 1 to 5 minutes

Figure 11.21

Purble Pairs

In this game shown in figure 11.22, your goal is to find all the matching pairs of pictures before time runs out. It is similar to the game Concentration.

- Number of players: 1
- Difficulty levels: Beginner, intermediate, advanced
- Typical playing time: 1 to 10 minutes

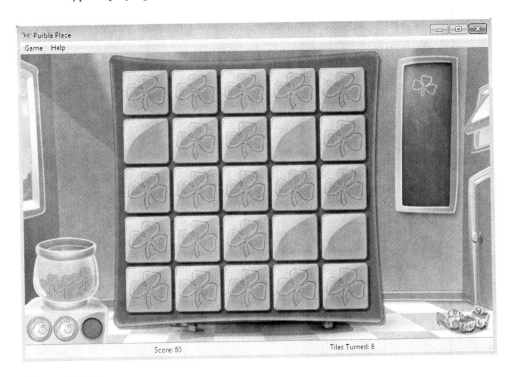

Figure 11.22

More Games!

Microsoft has a number of games by going to this URL:

http://zone.msn.com/en/root/gamebrowser.htm

This website allows you to download or play up to 1000 different games such as those shown in figure 11.23.

Bubble Town
Save Borb Bay from calamity in this addictive arcade-puzzler!

SCRABBLE® Blast
Connect letters on the board to make the longest possible words.

Bejeweled 2
Match gems to gain points in one of the most popular puzzle games of all time.

Figure 11.23

Notice in figure 11.24 from the same website that there are actually over 750 games you can download on to your Windows 7 computer.

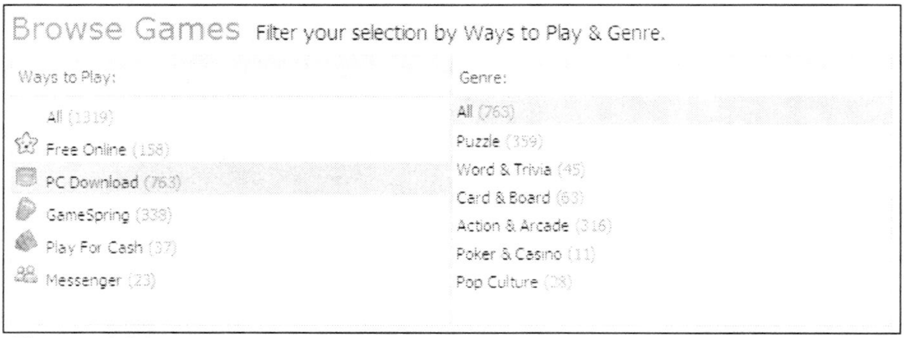

Browse Games Filter your selection by Ways to Play & Genre.

Ways to Play:	Genre:
All (1319)	All (763)
Free Online (158)	Puzzle (359)
PC Download (763)	Word & Trivia (45)
GameSpring (338)	Card & Board (63)
Play For Cash (37)	Action & Arcade (316)
Messenger (23)	Poker & Casino (11)
	Pop Culture (28)

Figure 11.24

Chapter 12 - Windows Media Player

Window Media Player in Windows 7 is new and improved. By default it is already pinned right on your Suberbar too as shown in Figure 12.1. It is the highlighted icon with the book and arrow pointing to the right.

Figure 12.1

The use features are generally the same as previous version except for a much glassier look. Since Windows 7 is focused around security, in this section we will learn about using customization to configure privacy options in Windows Media Player. Let's take a quick look at the new Windows Media Player as shown in figure 12.2.

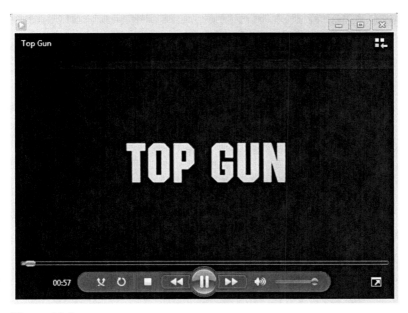

Figure 12.2

Libraries

Notice in the top right hand corner of the screen in figure 12.2 there are three boxes with an arrow. That is a button that will take you instantly to your Libraries. A new feature in Windows 7 and has its own icon on the Superbar by default which is the icon with a folder as shown in figure 12.1. Let's look at this new feature in figure 12.3.

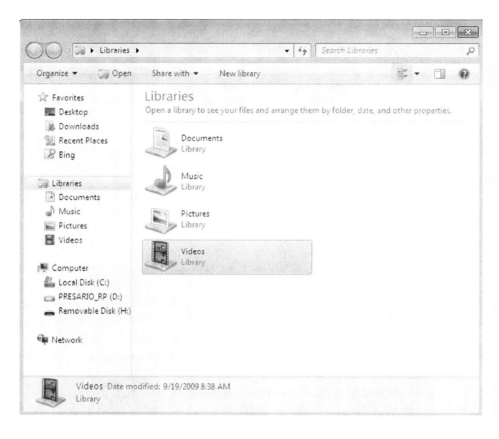

Figure 12.3

This is the new equivalent of Windows Explorer in Windows 7. In figure 12.4, let's take a more graphical look as this is the only way I think we can identify all the features of the Library.

Menu bar   Navigation   Library

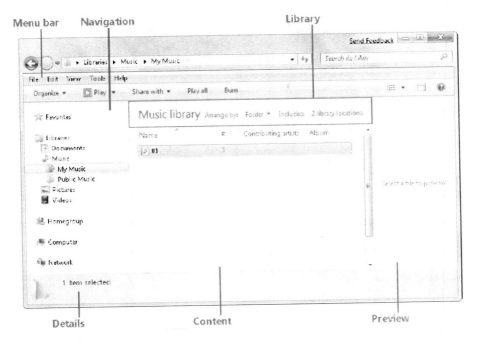

Details   Content   Preview

Figure 12.4

Windows Media Player Privacy Settings

Internet Explorer and many other programs gather and send data about what we do to people we don't know and without our knowledge. It almost makes me upset how many programs do this. And not always for marketing purposes either.

Now we can do something about it. To configure privacy settings, when setting up WMP11 for the first time, click on the Windows Media Player icon on the Superbar or go to Start, Programs, and Windows Media Player. Then select Custom Settings and click Next as shown in figure 12.5.

Figure 12.5

In figure 12.6 you can adjust the privacy options to your liking. Review the screenshot for my recommendations. The current settings shown are my personal recommendations.

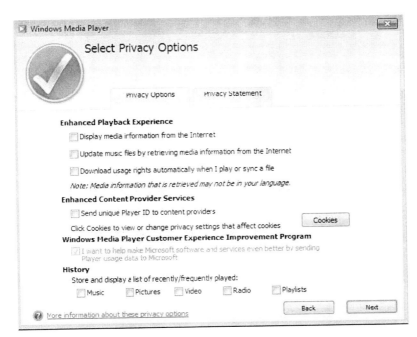

Figure 12.6

Once you are have started Windows Media Player you can adjust the Privacy Settings by right clicking on the display bar and choosing More Options, then the Privacy Tab as shown in figure 12.7.

Figure 12.7

With these settings your privacy is now protected when viewing and listening to media on the Internet or the local network.

Appendix A-Using Windows Easy Transfer

Windows Easy Transfer is just what it says, easy. You can use the Internet or go online and purchase an easy transfer cable. A standard USB cable will not work. You can also use an external USB or flash drive as well. The Windows Easy Transfer allows you to transfer profile settings such as the user accounts, documents, music, pictures, e-mail configuration settings, IE favorites, videos, desktop items, printer settings, and much more as shown in figure A.1.

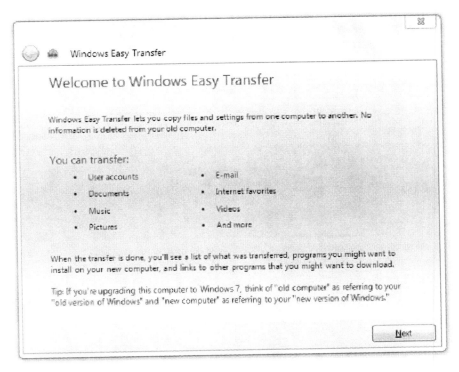

Figure A.1

Since I just went online and ordered my Easy Transfer Cable I won't have one to show you so I will use Windows Easy Transfer from my Vista laptop using the network I have here and make that selection in figure A.2.

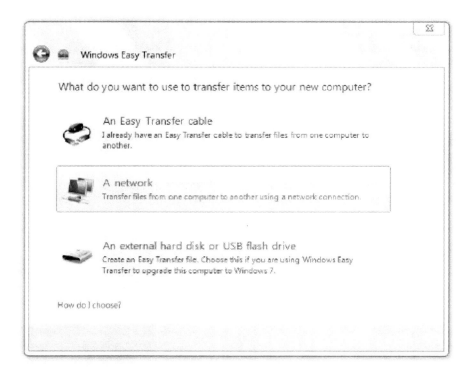

Figure A.2

After you choose the network selection, Windows 7 or Vista will give you a Windows Easy Transfer Key to use on the old PC you are transferring from as shown in figure A.3.

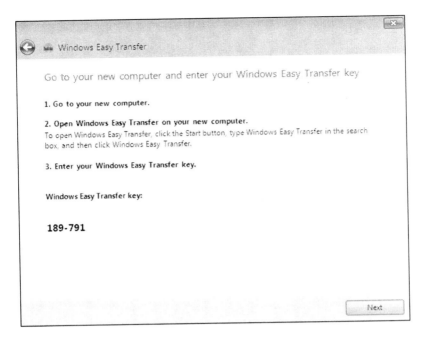

Figure A.3

Once you have entered the Windows Easy Transfer Key, it will automatically search the network for the new PC and transfer the profiles. This is not a quick transfer. This took about two hours for my profile containing about 2GB of files in the profiles.

Appendix B-Computer Management

The Computer Management console is used primarily for administrators but has some pretty nice features and can help you understand what is going on with your Windows 7 computer. In this section we will look at the following:

- Schedule a task
- Event Viewer
- Local Users and Groups
- Performance Monitor
- Device Manager
- Disk Management

Schedule a task

You must be logged on as an administrator account to perform these steps. If you use a specific program on a regular basis, you can use the Task Scheduler wizard to create a task that opens the program for you automatically. For example we have a server that needs to be rebooted at a certain time of the week, every Friday. That reboot can now be made an automated task as shown in figure B.1.

Figure B.1

To configure a Task, click the Action menu, and then click Create Basic Task. Type the name you want to use for the task. You can also enter an optional description, and then click Next.

> **NOTE:** *To select a schedule to run Daily, Weekly, Monthly, or One time, click Next; specify the schedule you want to use, and then click Next again.*
>
> *To schedule a task based on common recurring events, click, "When the computer starts", or "When you log on", and then click Next. If there are specific events, click "When a specific event is logged", click Next; specify the*

event log and other information using the drop-down lists, and then click Next.

To schedule a program to start automatically, simply select Start a program, and then click Next. Then click Browse to find the program you want to start, and then click Next again and then click Finish.

Event Logs

Event viewer as shown in figure B.2 is a viewer that allows you to read log files which are files that record events on your computer system including errors from programs, operating system errors, configuration errors, and user errors. Whenever these types of events occur, Windows records the event in an event log. The event log helps administrator find the detailed explanations of the cause of this issues.

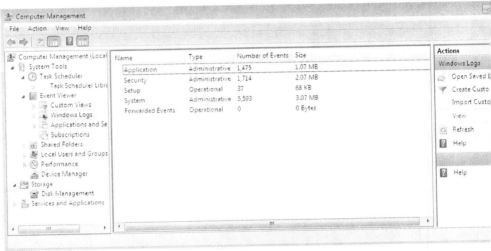

Figure B.2

Windows Logs include: classifies the system error events in to issues such as an error, warning, or information, depending on the severity of the event.

Local Users and Groups

Here you can create users that can log in to the computer or user accounts that can run services.

A user group is a collection user accounts can be a member of more than one security, global, or domain group. A user account is often referred to by the user group that it is in such as the administrator account. you can create custom user groups, move accounts from one group to another, and add or remove accounts from different groups. When you create a custom user group, you can choose which rights to assign.

You can create a user named Admin but until you add that user to the Administrators Group on the local PC he is a regular user with hardly any rights as shown in figure B.3.

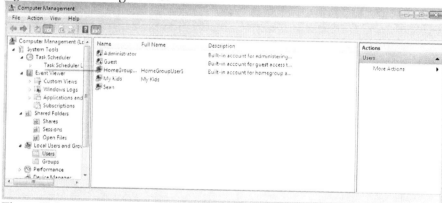

Figure B.3

258

Performance Monitor

Performance Monitor is found in Windows 7, Windows Server 2008 R2, and Windows Vista. It is a
powerful tool to help you visualize your PC's performance data in real time or from a log file. Performance Monitor allows you to examine the data it collects in a graph, histogram, or report as shown figure B.4. You can run Performance Monitor either on the PC or remotely from another PC or server.

ALERT: *Your user account must be included in the local Performance Log Users group to complete this procedure.*

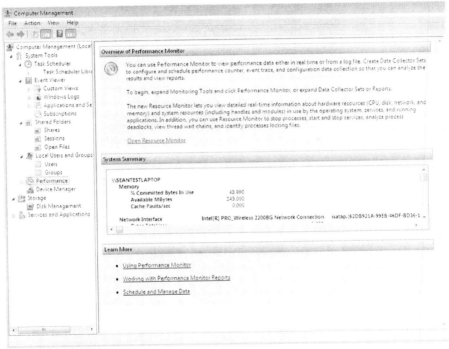

Figure B.4

Device Manager

Device Manager as shown in figure B.5 allows you to view and update the device drivers installed on your computer. You can also check to see if hardware is properly installed or modify the current hardware settings.

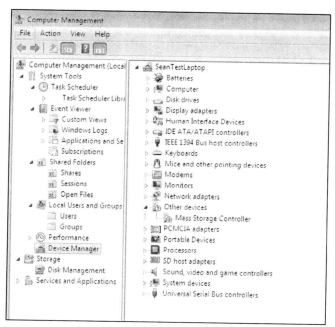

Figure B.5

NOTE: *You can open Device Manager: Click the Start button. In the search box, type Device Manager, and then, in the list of results, click Device Manager.*

Disk Management

Disk Manager as shown in figure B.6 is a utility that manages the system disks, volumes and partitions on the PC. With Disk Management, you can initialize disks; create volumes, format volumes with file systems FAT, exFAT, FAT32 or NTFS. You can also extend a disk, reduce a disk, check if a disk is healthy or unhealthy, create partitions, delete partitions, or change a drive letter.

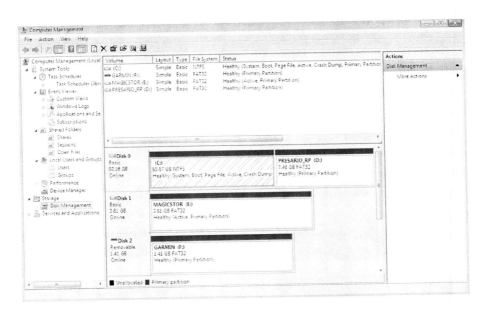

Figure B.6

> **Alert:** *Windows help does not have detailed information on how to use this feature. This topic is covered in detail in the Windows 7 Professional – The Little Black Book or you can see:*
>
> *http://windows7forums.com/windows-7-software/2076-disk-manager.html*

Appendix – C Creating Federated Search Connectors

I was on a blog the other day and someone wanted to know how to create a Federated Search Connector and here I writing a book about it. We got in to a discussion about how to configure it so I did some poking around Microsoft's site and found a nice article on how to create one. Since this book is about Microsoft I decided to do a search connector for Bing.com.

I first found information about deploying a Federated Search Tool at: http://msdn.microsoft.com/en-us/library/dd940454(VS.85).aspx#search_connector

Then I read up on deployment methods which made common sense at:. http://msdn.microsoft.com/en-us/library/dd940454(VS.85).aspx#fed_search_deployment

Then I stumbled on the magic link! A whole website pictured in figure C.1 and devoted just to configuring the search connector I wanted at: http://www.opensearch.org/Documentation/Developer_how_to_guide

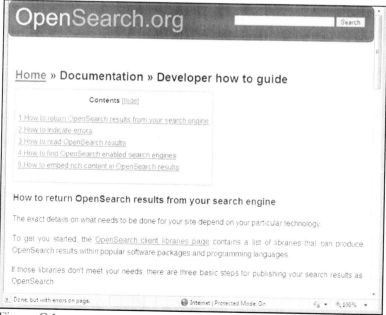

Figure C.1

There is too much information to put here in this section but I gave you the links to study. My code I developed is below and it took me about three hours to learn and develop. But if I had the links in the last page it probably would have taken me a half hour to develop. This code can be used by anyone as well.

```xml
<?xml version="1.0" encoding="UTF-8"?>
<OpenSearchDescription xmlns="http://a9.com/-/spec/opensearch/1.1/">
<ShortName>Bing Image Search</ShortName>
<Description>Seans Bing.com Federated Search Tool</Description>
<Tags>Image</Tags>
<LongName>bing.com Image Search</LongName>
<Image width="16" height="16"
type="image/gif">http://www.bing.com:80/s/rsslogo.gif</Image>
<Query role="example" searchterms="seattle"/>
<Developer>Microsoft Corporation, bing Search Development Team</Developer>
<SyndicationRight>limited</SyndicationRight>
<InputEncoding>UTF-8</InputEncoding>
<OutputEncoding>UTF-8</OutputEncoding>
<Url type="text/html" template="http://www.bing.com/images/search?q={searchTerms}"/>
<Url type="application/rss+xml"
template="http://api.bing.com/rss.aspx?source=image&amp;query={searchTerms}&amp;image.cou
nt=50&amp;mkt={language?}"/>
<ms-osc:ResultsProcessing format="application/rss+xml" xmlns:ms-
osc="http://schemas.microsoft.com/opensearchext/2009/">
<ms-osc:PropertyDefaultValues>
<ms-osc:Property schema="http://schemas.microsoft.com/windows/2008/propertynamespace"
name="System.PropList.ContentViewModeForSearch">prop:~System.ItemNameDisplay;System.Siz
e;~System.ItemPathDisplay</ms-osc:Property>
</ms-osc:PropertyDefaultValues>
</ms-osc:ResultsProcessing>
</OpenSearchDescription>
```

It took me about three hours to create the code for which I saved as Bing.osdx on the desktop after developing the code in Notepad. On the desktop as shown in figure C.2 you see the icon. Once you save .osdx file is ready to be emailed to anyone or placed as a download on your website. All someone has to do is double click or run the file on a Windows 7 PC.

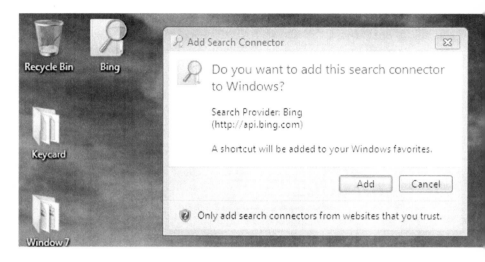

Figure C.2

Index

More titles from MediaWorks Publishing

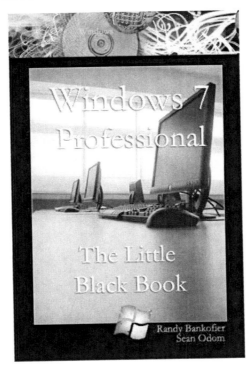

Windows 7 Professional
The Little Black Book
By: Randy Bankofier and Sean Odom

More Titles from Media Works

SEO For 2010: Search Optimization Secrets
By: Sean Odom and Sean R. Odom

CPSIA information can be obtained at www.ICGtesting.com
Printed in the USA
BVOW032119110712

294988BV00002BA/3/P

9 780557 137640